The 3D Printing
COOKBOOK

TINKERCAD EDITION

"David's after school class has been one of the most popular in the school and is always over-subscribed. This is because of his ease of communication and excellent method in teaching 3D printing. By developing the tasks as the ingredients of a recipe, with a step-by-step guide to produce a model, he has made the concepts accessible to all in a manageable way.

Dedicated in outlook, David is committed to the success of every child. I can definitely recommend David to you as a reliable and committed practitioner who motivates and inspires interest greatly in 3D printing."

- Brian Cooklin, Managing Director
Nord Anglia Education, India
(formerly Founding Principal of Nord Anglia
International School, Hong Kong)

"David's 3D printing class brings the future to life. Our young students are engaged and enthusiastic to learn skills in a subject that for their parents' generation will have seemed like science fiction."

- Ryan Speed, KS3 Computer Science Teacher
Nord Anglia International School Hong Kong

"I liked the 3D printing class because you learn a new thing. I also like it because it's something you can enjoy with your friends and family."

- Lili Dryden, age 9

"It was a great and fun experience getting to learn about 3D printing, as I was able to create many cool designs and enjoy making them at the same time."

- Mayu Okaguchi, age 9

"Learned a lot about new shapes and how to use the computer to create objects that were then printed for real. I loved seeing what I made on the screen actually become something I could bring home. I didn't know how to do any of this before starting the ECA so I learnt a lot. Mr. Seto was a great teacher with good information, tips and patience to help us create lots of cool and fun designs like astronauts, planes, cups and rockets!"

- Harry Kilmartin, age 10

"I took David Seto's 3D Printing for Beginners Workshop without any previous training. In just a short time, I was already doing 3D design on my own. Dave's teaching method is to make complicated things simple. His 3D Printing Cookbook distills his teaching methods into easy-to-follow recipes with pictures and step-by-step instructions that are clear and direct. Whether you are an adult learner or kid of any age (6-96!), there's something to learn from this cookbook."

- Hubie Lem, Vice Chair
Orion Astropreneur Space Academy

For Elizabeth, Katelyn, Jackson, Xiaoyan, Xiaojun, Alexandre, Yifu, Malcolm, and Connor — and future creators the world over...

The 3D Printing Cookbook
Text by David Seto
Design by Michael Welch

May 2021:   First Edition

Revision history for the First Edition:
2021-05-04: First release

See https://the3dprintingcookbook.com/tinkercad-edition for
release details.

ISBN: 978-1-7364982-8-6

The 3D Printing
COOKBOOK

TINKERCAD EDITION

3D design lessons
for 3D printing classes

—

in school,
after school
or home school

—

that don't involve just
3D printing name tags!

Text by David Seto
Design by Michael Welch

This book is ideal for children age 8 to 11.

For children older than 11, we recommend our companion book:

The 3D Printing Cookbook: Fusion 360 Edition

Contents

INTRODUCTION 1
Who Should Use This Book: 1
Why a Cookbook? 2
Book Structure 5
3D Printing Course Syllabus 6

GETTING SET UP 8
Student and Classroom Setup 8
  Classroom 9
  Overall Tools Checklist 9
  Tips for Running the Class 10
3D Design Software: Tinkercad 12
  Tinkercad for Teachers 15
Prepping a 3D Design for Printing 22
  Tips on Judging & Managing3D Designs before You Print 27
3D PrinterSetup and Use 30
  Setting up Your 3D Printer 30
  Using Your 3D Printer 32
  3D Printer Tools List 35

3D DESIGN: THE RECIPES 41
How did I decide on these designs? 41
Navigation 42
Table 51
Ring 63
Building 75
Cup 91
Heart-shaped Box 103
Toy Phone 119
Chocolate Bar 133
Robot Finger Tip 147
Rocket 161
Car 175
Wand 193

APPENDIX A: SYLLABUS & SLIDES 202
APPENDIX B: HANDOUTS FOR IN-CLASS USE 203
APPENDIX C: ADDITIONAL RESOURCES 219
APPENDIX D: GLOSSARY OF KEY 3D PRINTING TERMS 220
INDEX 224
KEY TOOLS CHEATSHEET 226
BASIC SHAPES CHEATSHEET 227

Note:

As with most software, Tinkercad gets updated intermittently. While we have tried our best to ensure our information is up-to-date, we do understand that software can be updated at any time which may result in small differences between the current state of the software and what we have presented in this book. Though the basic concepts will likely remain true for some time, we expect to update The 3D Printing Cookbook as the differences accumulate over time.

In the meantime, we hope you find this book both enjoyable and useful!

Introduction

Who Should Use This Book:

This book is absolutely, positively and definitely for you if you are:

- a school teacher new to STEAM subjects or are already teaching STEAM but lack the time to compile material related to 3D Printing
- a teacher just looking for a handful of 3D Printing projects to try out with your students
- a parent-teacher home schooling your children who's looking for STEAM-related learning projects (a truly commendable feat of dedication!)

This book targets educators new to 3D Printing. It uses Tinkercad (https://tinkercad.com), a freely available 3D modeling package from Autodesk which is the perfect 3D design tool for beginners. After going through the lessons in this book, your students will be able create their own 3D designs for 3D printing, not just replicate what you have already taught them.

Why a Cookbook?

Over the last three years, I have taught over 500 students, mostly ages 8-15 in after school programs, and I've come to appreciate the importance of establishing solid, relatable references. So, rather than solely communicating in 3D Printing tech jargon, like splines and vertices, I ask the students to take a big step back and look at it this way:

> "Making a 3D print is very similar to baking something in the oven. So I will teach you how to be a 3D Printing chef!"

Framing 3D Printing in this way has been very successful. The focus has always been to get the students as comfortable as possible using the 3D modeling tools so they can create designs on their own, just like when they would learn how to use ingredients to create a main dish and modify it based on their personal taste. As a result, my classes have been consistently oversubscribed, with one school term having 65 students signing up for 36 spots. By recreating a series of basic "entrees" the children grow to become very comfortable using over two dozen "ingredients" or 3D modeling tools by the end of the class to make their own masterpiece "dishes." You can see some of their results!

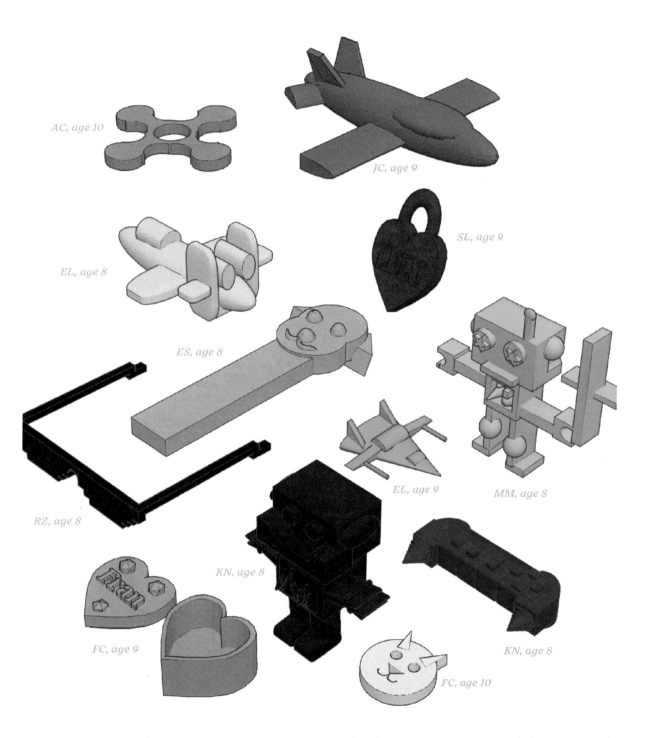

AC, age 10

JC, age 9

SL, age 9

EL, age 8

ES, age 8

RZ, age 8

EL, age 9

MM, age 8

KN, age 8

FC, age 9

KN, age 8

FC, age 10

Some "entrees" made by 8-10 year old
students during the class

David Seto & Michael Welch

Book Structure

With the "Cookbook" theme in mind, I have laid out this book in a step-by-step fashion so that you can transition into your school's best 3D printing teacher as smoothly as possible. Here are the chapters with a brief explanation on each.

Cooking	The 3D Printing Cookbook
Kitchen	**Student and Classroom setup** What you need, what's worked best for teaching kids, and a checklist for the things you need to get started.
Ingredients	**3D Design Software: Tinkercad** A quick introduction to the "ingredients" you will be using —namely Tinkercad.
Prep	**Prepping a 3D Design for 3D Printing** Here, I explain the necessary steps in preparing the "ingredients" just before you place the design in the "oven." This is similar to placing the ingredients in an oven-safe metal pan after you have combined the ingredients in a plastic bowl.
Oven	**3D Printer Setup and Use** We show you the ins and outs of your new 3D printing "oven" – types, capabilities, as well as some basic tips and troubleshooting.
Recipes	**The 3D Design "Recipes"** Here are the individual 3D design lessons for 3D printing to guide the students in making their first 3D design "dishes."

I also provide Appendices which include links to presentation materials for the class and a series of handouts for each design that your students use to test their newly acquired 3D modeling skills on their own.

3D Printing Course Syllabus

Here, let me show you how you can run a 3D Printing course, assuming 10-12 lessons:

Introduction to 3D printing
Sample 3D Prints
Navigation and moving

Recipe: Table
Recipe: Ring

Recipe: Building
Recipe: Cup
Challenge: Architecture / Kitchen

Recipe: Heart-shaped Box
Challenge: Decor

Recipe: Toy Phone
Challenge: Toys

Recipe: Chocolate Bar
Challenge: Food / Food Replicas / Student Projects[†]

Recipe: Robot Finger Tip
Challenge: Robotics / Student Projects[†]

Recipe: Rocket
Aerospace Challenge / Student Projects[†]

Recipe: Car
Automotive Challenge / Student Projects[†]

Recipe: Wand
Cosplay Challenge / Student Projects[†]

Creativity Challenge / Student Projects[†]

Creativity Challenge / Student Projects[†]

[†]*Student Projects are designs that students can create on their own.*

These are the lessons for each class. Between classes, you (or some of your students) can 3D print the models which meet the printing feasibility requirements that I will explain in more detail later in this book.

I hope this introduction has given you enough information to decide if this book is suitable for you or not. Of course, every teacher prefers to modify lessons to his or her personal style. But having spent a year building the content and then tweaking this course, I assure you this book will save you a lot of time.

Let's take a look!

Getting Set Up

Student and Classroom Setup

Should your students work in groups or individually?

In my experience, group projects are less ideal than individual projects, especially when the students are in the 8-10 year old range. Almost all my students have simply preferred to work on their own.

Doesn't that mean they are losing out on an opportunity to work in teams?

Yes, but I think that can come later. At this stage they are still learning the basics. I think it's fine they get comfortable with the modeling tools on their own before working together. So, ideally each student should have his or her own WiFi ready laptop or Chromebook to work with. (TinkerCad also runs well on iPads, and while the interface is the same, some of the interaction terminology may be different than that used in the lessons.)

Classroom

For the classroom, you will need:

1. a stable internet connection

2. an overhead projector to share your laptop screen with students so they can follow along with each step.

Beyond that, there are no other particularly special requirements. Your students sit as they usually do in a classroom, at their own desk and chair, with their own WiFi ready laptop. As you progress through each 3D model, the children will follow each of your mouse clicks, switching between your projected demonstration and their own laptop screen.

Overall Tools Checklist

☐ Tinkercad account for teachers and students (http://tinkercad.com)

☐ Laptops or Chromebooks with an internet browser for all the students

☐ Stable internet access

☐ Overhead projector with screen

☐ Handouts of the recipes in this book for each student

☐ Access to one or two 3D printers with some accessories

☐ 4-5 basic color filaments for the 3D printer

Tips for Running the Class

Before each class, take a few minutes to practice creating the models on your own. Even after teaching for three years, I still take a few minutes before each class to recreate the model I'm covering that day, just to make sure I can recreate the model smoothly when presenting to the students. If you know the mouse click sequences, you can complete most of the designs within three minutes.

Keep your class excited with 3D printing industry news and milestones. Here are some websites that cover what's happening in the 3D printing industry on a daily basis. While many are a bit too technical for younger students, some, like the first 3D printed human heart prototype, might inspire students to explore this new field! I generally visit the following sites at least once a week and often find something interesting, relevant or inspiring to share with the class.

- http://3dprint.com
- http://3dprintingindustry.com
- http://reddit.com/r/3dprinting

Inspire your students by bringing in designs printed in different materials. This can be done easily using an online service and may inspire students to experiment with printing more complex materials like metal, wood, ceramics — even chocolate! Seeing how one model reprinted with different materials is pretty amazing and really drives home one of the unique aspects of 3D printing.

Companies such as Shapeways can print your model using industrial 3D printers in dozens of different materials. I was very proud of one of my students who designed a small piece of jewelry for his mom and printed it in polished bronzed-silver steel. These companies offer various types of plastics, metals, very colorful sandstone and ceramic. Of course, pricing will depend on the material and size of the print. It takes about two weeks to complete a print and ship it to you.

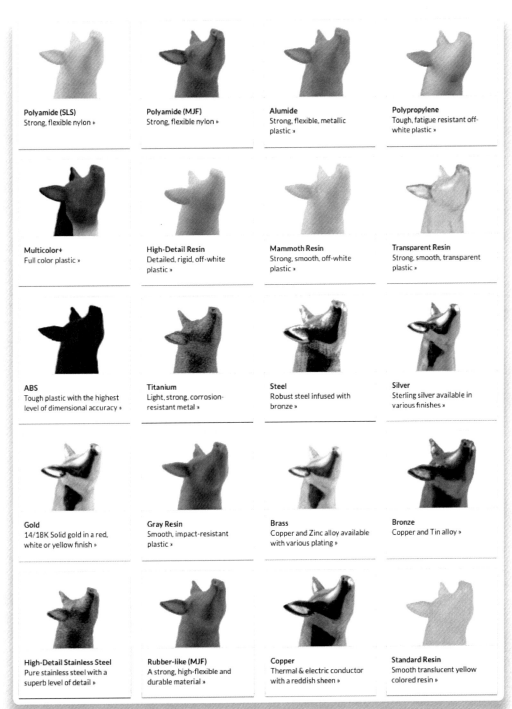

Polyamide (SLS)
Strong, flexible nylon »

Polyamide (MJF)
Strong, flexible nylon »

Alumide
Strong, flexible, metallic plastic »

Polypropylene
Tough, fatigue resistant off-white plastic »

Multicolor+
Full color plastic »

High-Detail Resin
Detailed, rigid, off-white plastic »

Mammoth Resin
Strong, smooth, off-white plastic »

Transparent Resin
Strong, smooth, transparent plastic »

ABS
Tough plastic with the highest level of dimensional accuracy »

Titanium
Light, strong, corrosion-resistant metal »

Steel
Robust steel infused with bronze »

Silver
Sterling silver available in various finishes »

Gold
14/18K Solid gold in a red, white or yellow finish »

Gray Resin
Smooth, impact-resistant plastic »

Brass
Copper and Zinc alloy available with various plating »

Bronze
Copper and Tin alloy »

High-Detail Stainless Steel
Pure stainless steel with a superb level of detail »

Rubber-like (MJF)
A strong, high-flexible and durable material »

Copper
Thermal & electric conductor with a reddish sheen »

Standard Resin
Smooth translucent yellow colored resin »

Material samples from i.materialize.com - an 3D printing service provider

3D Design Software: Tinkercad

For children 8 to 11 years old, I recommend teaching Tinkercad. Why Tinkercad? Three main reasons:

It's free. Created by Google engineers back in 2010, Tinkercad (http://tinkercad.com) has been part of the Autodesk suite of computer-assisted-design (CAD) software since 2013. Autodesk's main customer base are industrial manufacturers but they have a dedicated team maintaining Tinkercad with regular updates. The software giant (US$3.3bn in revenue in 2020) has had a long standing policy of providing all their software free to schools. Tinkercad is special because it's just free to use all the time, whether or not the user is in school.

Released by ex-Googlers in 2010.

Backed by industry leader – Autocad.

Free for public use.

Geared toward classroom.

Suitable for beginners and intermediate learners alike.

https://tinkercad.com

Autodesk believes in Tinkercad's mission to make 3D modeling, especially the design of physical items, accessible to the general public. Given this, it should be safe to say:

1. Tinkercad is here to stay

2. Tinkercad will likely remain free for public use for the foreseeable future as it's Autodesk's entry point to learning 3D modeling.

It's geared to classroom education. Just introduced in the fall of 2019, the Tinkercad Classroom offers a more streamlined approach for children to access Tinkercad without the need to creating their own account. (Children under 14 actually need parental approval to sign up for an account.) The teacher, using his or her own account, just displays a Class Code which the children can all use to log in. The teacher can then manage the entire class in one location in Tinkercad. The next section will provide a step-by-step guide to the process.

It's very suitable for beginners and intermediate level users. Tinkercad is extremely popular among my 8 to 11 year-old students. We often end a class session where a handful of students are absolutely torn between working on their model or running off to catch their bus!

While it might be reasonable to assume that older kids will pick up Tinkercad faster than younger children, I have seen many 8-year olds outperform 11-year olds. Patience and perseverance are important factors.

Here is a slide I always share with the students in the first class to help them better understand the differences between the amount of effort required for different results:

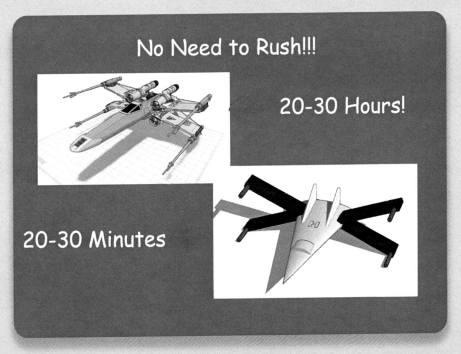

Tinkercad can create some really sophisticated designs, but you need to take it one step at a time.

David Seto & Michael Welch

Tinkercad for Teachers

How to set yourself up as a teacher in Tinkercad

Create an account for yourself on tinkercad.com, using Join Now on the home page...

...and register yourself as a teacher with Educators start here on the second page.

Then enter your details to complete setting up your account.

Start Tinkering

How will you use Tinkercad?

In school?

Educators start here

Students, join a Class

On your own

Create a personal account

Already have an account?
Sign In

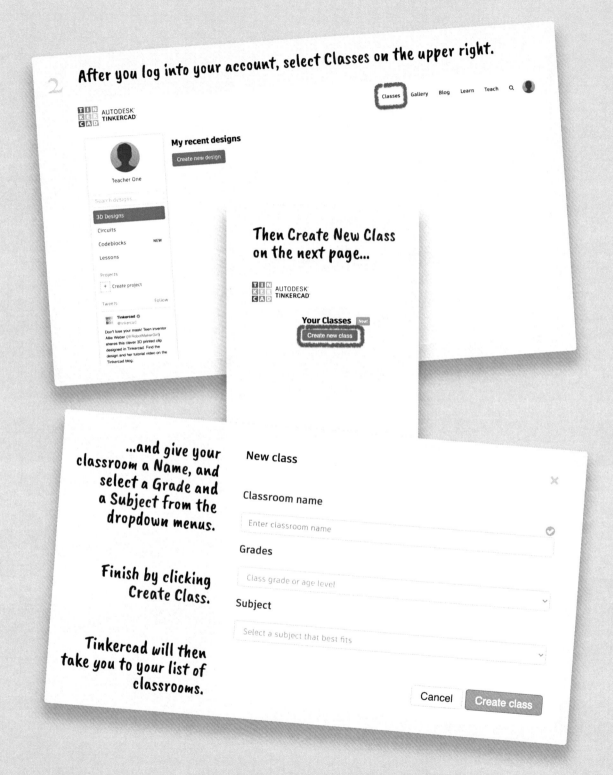

2

After you log into your account, select Classes on the upper right.

Classes   Gallery   Blog   Learn   Teach

My recent designs

Create new design

Teacher One

Search designs

3D Designs

Circuits

Codeblocks   NEW

Lessons

Projects

+   Create project

Tweets   Follow

Tinkercad
@tinkercad
Don't lose your mask! Teen inventor
Allie Weber (@RobotMakerGirl)
shares this clever 3D printed clip
designed in Tinkercad. Find the
design and her tutorial video on the
Tinkercad blog.

Then Create New Class
on the next page...

Your Classes New!

Create new class

...and give your
classroom a Name, and
select a Grade and
a Subject from the
dropdown menus.

Finish by clicking
Create Class.

Tinkercad will then
take you to your list of
classrooms.

New class   ✕

Classroom name

Enter classroom name   ✓

Grades

Class grade or age level

Subject

Select a subject that best fits

Cancel   Create class

3 **Find the classroom that you just created, click it to enter, and begin to populate it with the names of your students.**

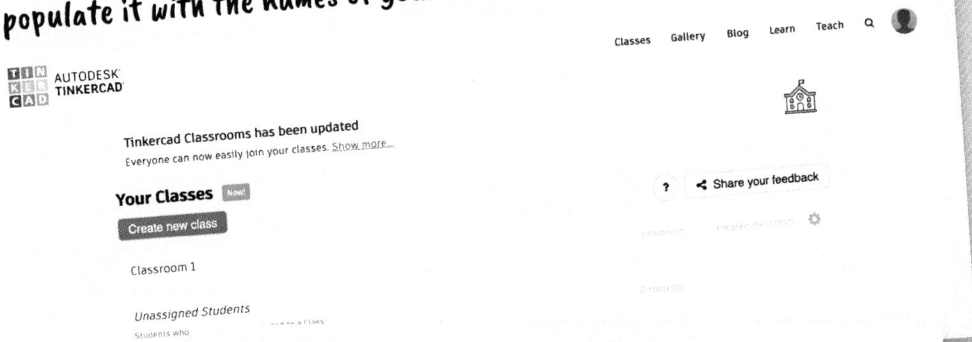

Classes Gallery Blog Learn Teach 🔍

AUTODESK
TINKERCAD

Tinkercad Classrooms has been updated
Everyone can now easily join your classes. Show more...

? ◁ Share your feedback

Your Classes New!

Create new class

Classroom 1

Unassigned Students
Students who...

Populate your class by selecting Add students.

Here you can add students one by one or you can paste a list of their names.

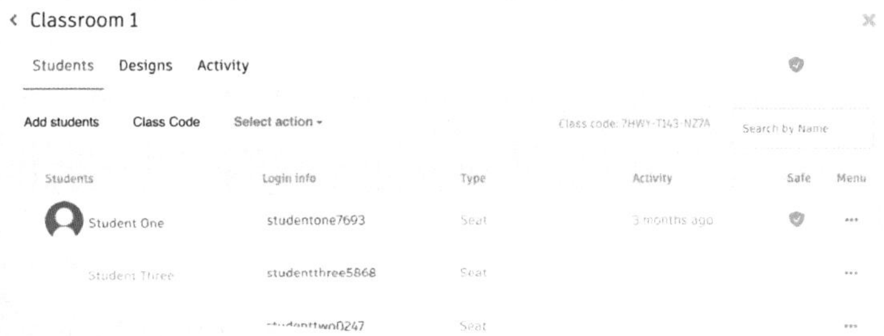

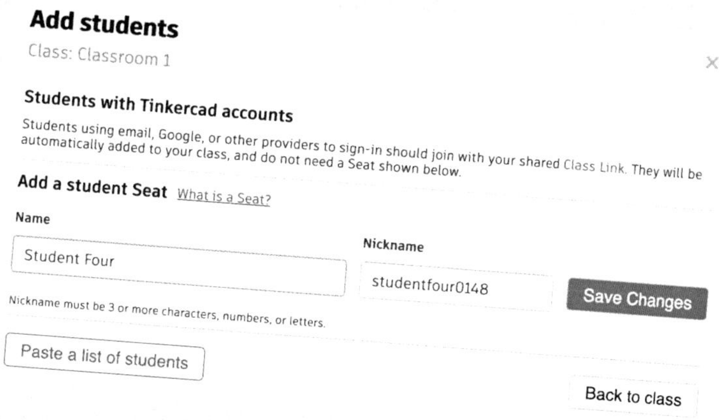

‹ Classroom 1   ✕

Students Designs Activity   🛡️

Add students   Class Code   Select action ▾   Class code: 7HW9-T143-NZ7A   Search by Name

Students	Login info	Type	Activity	Safe	Menu
👤 Student One	studentone7693	Seat	3 months ago	✓	•••
Student Three	studentthree5868	Seat			•••
	studenttwo0247	Seat			•••

Add students
Class: Classroom 1   ✕

Students with Tinkercad accounts
Students using email, Google, or other providers to sign-in should join with your shared Class Link. They will be automatically added to your class, and do not need a Seat shown below.

Add a student Seat What is a Seat?

Name

| Student Four |

Nickname

| studentfour0148 | Save Changes

Nickname must be 3 or more characters, numbers, or letters.

Paste a list of students

Back to class

Tinkercad will automatically create a Nickname for each student.

Make sure your students can see this list of nicknames with their own corresponding name at the start of each class.

Click Back to Class when done.

4 From here, you should be able to see the names of all your students with their Tinkercad Nicknames. Click Class Code at the top of the class list.

‹ Classroom 1   ✕

Students   Designs   Activity

Add students   Class Code   Select action ▾   Class code: 7HWY-T143-NZ7A   Search by Name

	Login info	Type	Activity	Safe	Menu
Students					
👤 Student One	studentone7693	Seat	3 months ago	✓	•••
Student Four	studentfour0148	Seat			•••
Student Three	studentthree5868	Seat			•••
Student Two	studenttwo0247	Seat			•••

At the start of each class, make sure your students can see this code on your projector screen as that's how they will join your classroom.

Log in to Classroom 1 with:

7HWY T143 NZ7A

[Copy code]   [Copy link]

Student instructions
Have a class link?
1. Go to your class at https://www.tinkercad.com/**joinclass**/7HWYT143NZ7A.
2. Enter the **Nickname** your teacher assigned you.

Have a class code?
1. Go to https://www.tinkercad.com/**joinclass**
2. Enter your class code: **7HWYT143NZ7A**
3. Enter the **Nickname** your teacher assigned you.

5 Have the students open up https://www.tinkercad.com on an internet browser and ask them to click Join your class on the bottom right of the main page.

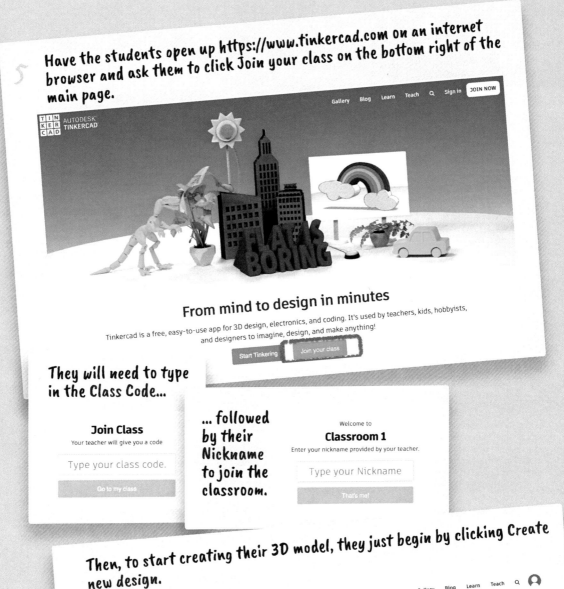

They will need to type in the Class Code...

Join Class

Your teacher will give you a code

Type your class code.

Go to my class

... followed by their Nickname to join the classroom.

Welcome to

Classroom 1

Enter your nickname provided by your teacher.

Type your Nickname

That's me!

Then, to start creating their 3D model, they just begin by clicking Create new design.

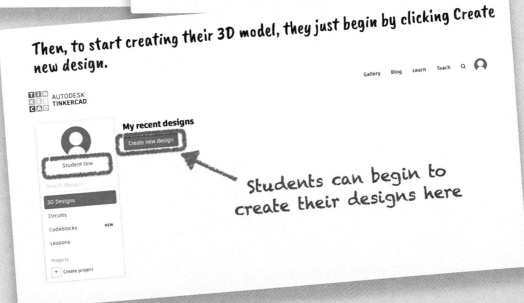

Students can begin to create their designs here

6 After the students finish creating their 3D designs, you, as their teacher, can access their models by going into their classroom by clicking Classes...

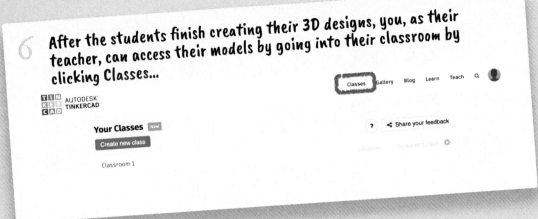

...then click the student's name...

Students who created a design highlighted in blue; click to access

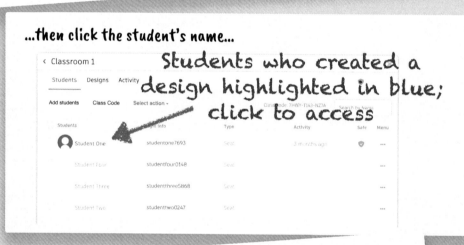

...and now you can open any of their designs to modify or export for printing!

Click to access any specific design

Prepping a 3D Design for Printing

When we want to print a paper document like a PDF file, we just locate the Print button, click and you can pick up your document at the printer a few seconds later. The 3D printing process is not that simple nor as fast, but I'm sure it will improve dramatically in the coming years if not sooner.

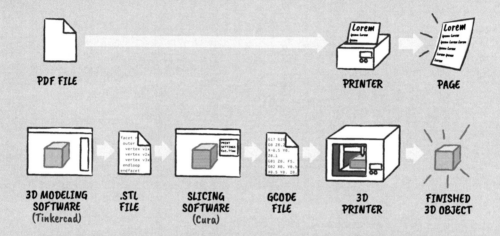

There are two issues that currently complicate the 3D printing process:

- You need to convert your 3D model (usually an STL file) into a file format that most 3D printers can read and execute (usually a G-code file —more on G-code files later on.)

- Even if a new file format was created that would skip the STL-to-G-code conversion process, that format would have to be widely adopted by 3D software developers and printer manufacturers before we can have a true print-and-go process like 2D paper printers. That doesn't mean it's not going to happen, it'll just take time.

Some 3D printers, like MakerBot, come with their own proprietary conversion software (called a slicer) — but these are more the exception than the rule.

In the meantime, here are the steps to 1) export a Tinkercad model and 2) convert it into a G-code file for 3D Printing.

1. When you believe a model is ready for printing, click Export.

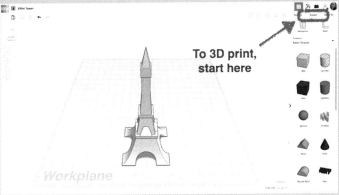

To 3D print, start here

2. Next you need to decide if you want to Download the file or Send it to an outside 3D printing service provider for printing. (I usually select Download because I have access to a 3D printer.) If I only have one model on the Workplane, I just select Everything in the

design. If I have more than one model on the Workplane, I make sure I have selected that model and choose the Selected shapes option (you need to select something first). I choose STL exclusively and Tinkercad will ask where to download the STL file, which is usually a file folder on my desktop labeled with the date.

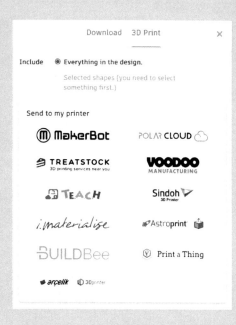

3. If you prefer to send the design to a professional 3D printing service company, Tinkercad gives you some options such as MakerBot and Polarcloud.

4. Now you will use your STL file to create a G-code file for the 3D printer — don't worry, you don't need to learn how to code for this! The G-code file will slice your model into a series of stacked layers, much like a deck of cards, and includes a set of instructions that tells the 3D printer what to do and how to operate.

G-code instructions tell the printer what to print on each of the 2D layers, including where to print the support material and how to print the infill for each model. If you plan to print multiple models at the same time, then you will need to include all of them in one G-code file by importing each into your slicer and laying them out on the slicer's virtual print bed.

5. Setting up a G-code file can be as simple as using the basic default settings, or it can be very detailed if you're trying to optimize for speed, strength, or other factors. Here are some screen shots from Cura, the very popular free slicing software which you can download from: https://ultimaker.com/software/ultimaker-cura. Please note that a detailed discussion of Cura or other slicing software is beyond the scope of this book. However, I will give you some basic pointers which you can use immediately to 3D print using Cura.

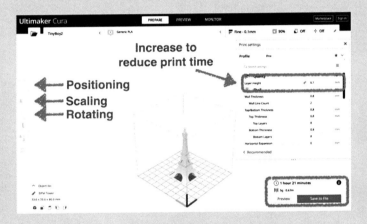

6. After I load my 3D model's STL file into the Cura slicer software to create a G-code file, I can make adjustments to it with the settings on the left side of the screen. Scaling is the most important one as I usually want to limit the size of the print to something close to the size of a tennis ball. Most slicer software can estimate the print time as you make each change —this you can see in the lower-right corner of the Cura window. The estimated printing time is also a function of which 3D printer you are using and how fast it prints.

7. You can make hundreds of minor adjustments to the slicer settings, but the one setting I always use is the Layer Height. Increasing the Layer Height gives the model a rougher feel than if we kept it at the 0.1mm default setting, but it can cut the print time in half —which is important if you have a dozen prints to do each week. I often use 0.3mm and the students seem to like their prints just fine.

Cura has an online discussion forum if you want to explore this further. I'm sure other slicer software have their own discussion forums as well. Please see Appendix C Additional Resources for more information.

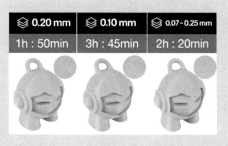

8. When you have decided on the slicer settings that will work best for you, just Save to File. This will create the G-Code file, which you will send to your 3D Printer. For my printers, I copy the G-code to a mini SD card, which I then transfer to the 3D printer.

Tips on Judging & Managing 3D Designs before You Print

It is important to note that not all 3D models are printable. Ideally every student follows your instructions and knows how to use the tools without error, but realistically there will be a small number of models the printer won't be able to reproduce in the real world. As an instructor, it's important for you to understand why so you can help teach your students to avoid these problems.

Frequently, these simple problems are often physics-related or may occur due to tricks of perception when viewing from different angles, for example:

1) a section that is **too thin or steeply angled** to print and will break quickly once it comes off the 3D printer

2) a section that's **literally floating in 3D space** (I call them Floaters) or is not attached to anything

3) a section that's clearly **improperly aligned** but student submitted for printing because he or she had to catch the bus. A lot of these issues are easy to fix once you see them, so it is important to teach students to view their models from different perspectives and think about some of the different

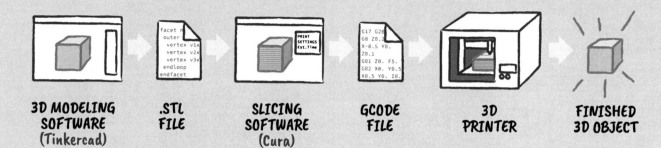

3D MODELING SOFTWARE (Tinkercad) → **.STL FILE** → **SLICING SOFTWARE** (Cura) → **GCODE FILE** → **3D PRINTER** → **FINISHED 3D OBJECT**

physical limitations of their work. Because you want the students to learn, you should have them correct the error before they have you print it.

Use a tennis ball as the default size of the 3D prints. Tennis balls are almost 7cm (2.7in) in diameter. This is a good size for most children to hold in their hands. Depending on the complexity of the model and the slicer settings, expect each model to take about 45 minutes on average (give or take 15 minutes).

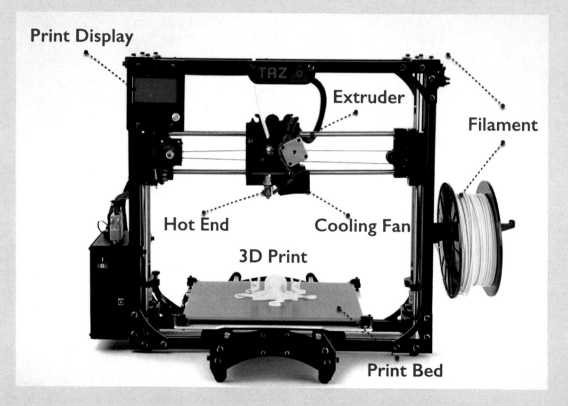

Print Display

Extruder

Filament

Hot End

Cooling Fan

3D Print

Print Bed

Take advantage of the default settings in your slicer software. Many slicing software have default settings specially tailored for your 3D printer. There are about a dozen core settings in most 3D printers that control factors like the temperature of the print nozzle, the nozzle speed and adhesion method to the print bed. But for your first set of prints, just start with the default settings. They might be all you ever need.

When preparing for a batch print of 10 or more models at once, try to find the optimum number of models that your 3D printer can handle in one go. If your students are creating models at a frantic pace, as mine have, I end up needing to 3D print as many as 30 models by the next week. You will be tempted to load your 3D printer with as many models as possible to minimize the number of batch prints — just be aware that your printer will likely push back when it's overloaded, resulting in failed prints, and stopping or jamming in the middle of the night. My CR10, which has a 300mm square print bed, can handle about 12 models at once.

3D Printer
Setup and Use

Setting up Your 3D Printer

While my class is called "The 3D Printing ECA" (Extracurricular Activity), there is a simple reality that we need to face: today's 3D printers print very slowly. Going back to my cooking analogy, it's more like baking in a traditional oven instead of using a microwave. Because the process is slow, I rarely run 3D prints during class except to demonstrate the printing process. A tennis ball-sized object will take about 30-45 minutes to print which is already half the typical class time.

Besides, once you start a 3D print, it really is similar to watching cookies baking in the oven; it's interesting for about two minutes but then you're ready to move on to the next thing. Typically I'll demonstrate a print in the first class, but in subsequent classes, children will spend most of their time designing and I will print their designs before the next class. This explains why my 3D printers are set up against the back wall of a classroom instead of at the center.

A large sized 3D printer — Generally, I use a 3D printer that can print 10-12 tennis ball-sized models at once at a relatively decent quality. Specifically, the printing space (or volume) of my 3D printer is 300mm by 300mm by 400mm, which is width, depth and height respectively. In effect, I am running a small factory because I run the 3D printer in batches.

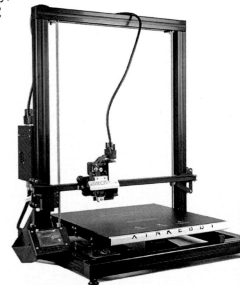

After a class, I vet the students' finished models. For a class of 12 students, there are usually at least 10 models that I deem print worthy. (*See **Tips on Judging and Managing 3D Designs Before You Print** in the previous section.*) These models go into a queue which I send to the 3D printer before I head home. The models will print over night and can be retrieved the next morning. (*Please see **Using Your 3D Printer** in the next section*) For my classes, I need to complete the prints before the start of the next class, which is usually a week later. For multiple classes of 12 students each, I would print 20-30 prints for that week. By the end of the course, my main 3D printer will have produced about 150 prints for the school term (or 300 per school year).

A smaller backup 3D printer — While the children are usually quite content with getting their 3D print in a single color of my choosing, some will have more specific requests which I also try to accommodate. For example, one very dedicated student wanted to print a heart shaped box in one color, but a highly decorative lid in another color for her mom's birthday. This is when a small backup 3D printer comes in very handy. I can print one part of her model along with the other student models in the large batch print, while the lid can be done in the smaller printer. This saves a lot of time by avoiding the need to switch filaments. Note that these requests are not very common, perhaps one in 75 models, but I try to satisfy them when the occasion arises. Another reason for having a smaller backup printer is in case the large printer produces a faulty print, I can use the backup printer to redo it — but this is also relatively rare.

Using Your 3D Printer

Here's what you need to know to run a 3D printer. While there are many different 3D printers in the market, the information here should be enough to get you started. Troubleshooting for any specific 3D printer is outside the scope of this book, so please refer to your 3D printer's customer support website, Google, or an online forum to address printer specific issues.

Find a stable platform, away from direct sunlight. You want a stable platform because the print bed in your 3D printer needs to be as perfectly level and as still as possible to ensure good prints. I've run a batch of prints where the left side prints were okay but the models on the right turned out compressed because the print bed was tilting to the left. If your table is also wobbly, it will just compound the problem. You'll also want to avoid positioning your printer in direct sunlight because, in addition to the potential damage on the printer's machinery, your plastic filament spool will deteriorate faster as well, which will affect the overall quality of your prints.

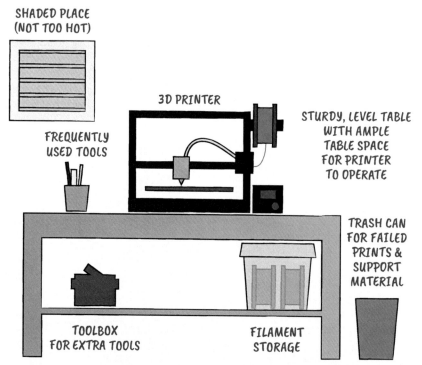

SHADED PLACE (NOT TOO HOT)

3D PRINTER

STURDY, LEVEL TABLE WITH AMPLE TABLE SPACE FOR PRINTER TO OPERATE

FREQUENTLY USED TOOLS

TRASH CAN FOR FAILED PRINTS & SUPPORT MATERIAL

TOOLBOX FOR EXTRA TOOLS

FILAMENT STORAGE

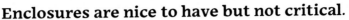

Enclosures are nice to have but not critical. While it's generally a good idea to use a 3D printer that's fully enclosed when there are many children around due to the 200° C (392° F) temperature of the plastic filament extruder, I have yet to encounter a situation where children have disturbed a print run, even ones that run all day. Most children are fascinated by the process and just watch for a few minutes before heading off to their next class. This is beneficial because most of the larger 3D printers suitable for schools have no enclosures.

Make sure you have space for storing extra filament spools, small tools and support material. For a school year with about 20-24 classes of 36 students, I have found that five rolls of 1-kg filament is enough to cover all their prints, which will run close to 300 prints. You'll need storage space for these rolls. You also need to store the tools that come with the 3D printer, although my personal favorite tool is my trusty Swiss Army pocket knife which I use to remove prints that may get stuck on the print bed. Tools will vary depending on the 3D printer you have, but might include a spatula, Allen wrenches, extra nuts and bolts, perhaps even a wrench to disassemble the extruder head assembly.

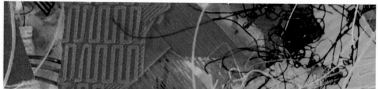

Recycled PLA support material —you'll have a lot of it! \ source: all3dp.com

You will also need a box for discarded support material, the thinner layers of plastic that hold up over-hanging parts of any design, like scaffolds. Imagine a robot with an outstretched arm; the slicing software will automatically detect that. Printing out filament in mid air won't work when it gets to arm height, so it lays down a tower of support material. When it begins to print the arm, the arm will have the support material to hold up the incoming print. After the print is done, you or your students will want to remove the support material in order to expose the final model.

The overhangs in the letter Y do not require 3D printing support structures. The ones in the letter T do require them. \ source: 3DHubs

This support material can be reused in other forms including being remelted into new spools of filament. I have yet to explore this space but it is certainly on my research short list.

Expect occasional maintenance work. The print bed should be clean. Baby wipes or wet paper towels followed by dry paper towels generally work well. If I used glue sticks to help adhere the prints, then baby wipes are usually very useful at removing any residue.

The bigger issue is the print head or extruder. Depending on how old your filament is or if a part of the extruder has slipped out of alignment, you might find that the printer has jammed mid-print. Ideally, if the warranty is still valid, you can send it in for repairs (hence it's good to have a back-up printer). If not, then the next best thing is to find an online community where you can seek help. In the last three years, I've experienced both situations with my Creality CR-10S. In one case, the manufacturer shared a video showing me how to recalibrate the extruder. In the other, I just bought a new extruder.

3D Printer Tools List

As the quality of 3D printers improve over time, you will find that you probably won't need many of these tools. But I've listed them based on my experience using 3D printers over the last few years.

Glue stick, hair spray, or blue tape. You always want the 3D printer's extruder head to be 1/10th of a millimeter (0.0039 inch) away from the print bed over the entire surface of the print bed. That's about the thickness of a sheet of paper. Sometimes, perhaps even due to changes in humidity, the print bed is off slightly and the print might actually peal off the print bed mid print, which will require a complete reprint. When this happens, I apply a thin layer of glue from a glue stick to ensure the base of the print will stay in place throughout the printing process. I can always clean the print bed afterwards with a wet paper towel. Just dry the surface afterwards with a new paper towel and you're ready to tackle the next batch.

Work gloves. You definitely want to protect your hands when your prints are stuck on the print bed and you're slicing away with a spatula or pocket knife. Please believe me when I tell you I have had my share of blood drawn due to a run away pocket knife during a print extraction.

Spatula or pocket knife. To help you remove the prints from the print bed if they get stuck.

Needle nose pliers. These will help a lot when the prints have support material to be removed.

Allen wrenches. Over time your 3D printer will need minor tightening as nuts and bolts become loose with use. Of course be aware that this might void your warranty, so proceed with caution.

Extra nuts and bolts. These might come with the 3D printer as spare parts.

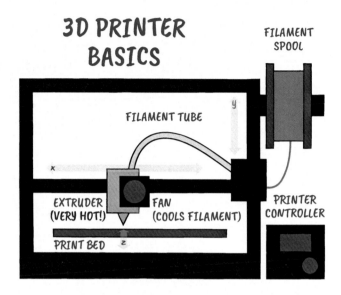

3D PRINTER BASICS

FILAMENT SPOOL

FILAMENT TUBE

y

x

EXTRUDER (VERY HOT!)   FAN (COOLS FILAMENT)

PRINT BED   z

PRINTER CONTROLLER

Ensure the 3D printer's extruder maintains a consistent distance from and throughout the print bed. This is the best way to get consistently good prints and is especially so for printers with adjustable foot pegs. During a print, the extruder is pushing out filament, if it gets too close to the print bed your print will likely jam the extruder; if the distance is too far, your print might develop wobbly vertical faces.

Most 3D printers have already been calibrated to that "not so high, not so low" sweet spot. Missing that sweet spot is one main reason why prints fail. If you get a 3D printer with adjustable foot pegs, you should learn the "paper sheet thickness test." This might sound overly troublesome, but please don't worry. With some practice, it becomes secondary. Just run the "level the bed" function on the printer which will start a five point check where the extruder head moves to the center and four corners of the print bed. At each point, place a sheet a paper between the extruder and the print bed. If you can pull out the sheet and feel a "small" tug, then the distance is in the sweet spot. If not, you will need

The "Magical" Piece of Paper

to adjust the foot pegs until you reach that point. This process should take less than five minutes and, again, this test is mainly for printers with foot pegs adjusters.

Use glue sticks, hair spray or blue tape if your prints are not sticking to the print bed. This may or may not be an issue depending on the quality of your 3D printer, but if your 3D prints never complete because they slide around the print bed while printing, you will want to explore one of these options. I have found glue sticks have worked best for me when this issue arises.

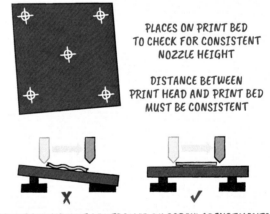

PLACES ON PRINT BED TO CHECK FOR CONSISTENT NOZZLE HEIGHT

DISTANCE BETWEEN PRINT HEAD AND PRINT BED MUST BE CONSISTENT

Set aside some time to remove support material from your prints. Needle-nose pliers are my tool of choice for removing support material.

PRINT BED HEIGHT CONTROLLED BY SCREW ADJUSTMENTS

Consider getting a webcam or an Octoprint (octoprint.org) to monitor the printing process for your overnight prints. Some 3D printers, like the MakerBot, have a webcam already installed, but most do not. Having the ability to watch the print build process should provide some peace of mind and you'll know what to expect when you return to your printer the next day. You can also record a time-lapse video to show in class so students can see printing successes and failures.

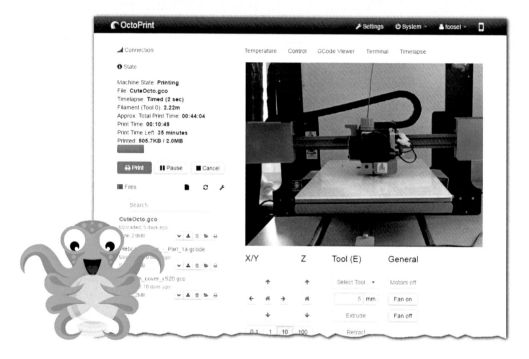

Be prepared for minor adjustments to some 3D printers, with one big repair (see next tip) some time in the future. While most 3D printers on the market today are generally stable, well-balanced machines, at the end of the day they are still machines prone to wear and tear. After heavy usage, say by your 300th print, you might find that the extruder might be clogging or the filament is not rolling as smoothly as it used to. If your warranty is still valid you should certainly contact the distributer or manufacturer. Most 3D printer manufacturers already have trouble-shooting information on their websites so it will be your call on whether or not you can make the adjustment yourself or wait for the repair staff. This could be as simple as sliding a cleaning needle into the extruder head to unclog the channel. But it's best to talk to the manufacturer first.

Back in 2014, I took a weekend to assemble an early model 3D printer kit by myself- a Printrbot Jr. That experience alone has given me an understanding of the basic parts of most 3D printers —even though I don't know the details of each one. I strongly encourage you to also find a small 3D printer assembly kit and give it a try! Certain adjustments to your 3D printer might be very simple and can be done on your own. Just double check with the manufacturer before you proceed.

A Printrbot Jr from 2014 \ Courtesy Printrbot's Brook Drumm

Your biggest repair on your 3D printer will likely be replacing the entire extruder assembly. Depending on your 3D printer, there's a good chance your printer nozzle will jam from the accumulation of the filament residue after several hundred hours of print time. This is actually very common. If repeated cleaning of the nozzle fails, then it would probably be best to just buy a new assembly. This becomes really obvious when your printer repeatedly prints out "bowls of spaghetti" or a sizable blob of molten plastic.

For those on a tight financial budget, you don't really need to buy your own 3D printer. If you search online for "3D Printing Service" in your neighborhood, you should be able to find something available. Also consider checking out the local public library. The downside is they might take more time given their potential backlogs. So you can consider using them for large final projects.

David Seto & Michael Welch

3D DESIGN: THE RECIPES

I hope you find these models as useful as I have when teaching 3D modeling for 3D printing. Once again, the overall goal is to get the students familiar and comfortable enough with the design tools in order to create their own models. We want them to become their own 3D printing chefs! Each design covers a half dozen design tools or more, so the students can learn by exposure to new tools as well as through iteration.

How did I decide on these designs?

Each model represents an industry that 3D printing technology is affecting today. For example, the building represents the architecture industry, the rocket for aerospace, and the chocolate bar for food. You can easily find examples of each with a quick on-line search. But I suspect you will also find industries that I've not covered here, which only means the list is growing! I believe this is a very strong reason for us to teach our children 3D design for 3D printing at an age as early as possible to help them in their future professional endeavors.

Navigation

START HERE

This should be your first lesson in Tinkercad because it provides an overview of how to get around the software. While the students are likely already familiar with running through a 3D video game, which gives them a 3D perspective, the Navigation and Move tools in Tinkercad are more refined. For example, you can rotate an object by just 0.5 degrees if needed. (OK it's not used much, but you get the idea.) To run this first class, just drag a red box onto the Workplane and go through each of the Navigation and Move tools.

Create new design: After you and all your students have logged in, Tinkercad will take you to your Dashboard. Just click Create new design to begin.

Your Dashboard

Gallery   Blog

AUTODESK
TINKERCAD

My recent designs

Create new design

Student One

3D Designs

Circuits

Codeblocks   NEW

Lessons

Projects

+ Create project

Click here to
make a
new design

2   The Workplane: The main workspace is called the Workplane, which features very useful grid lines both large and small. Across the top, there are two areas you and your students need to be aware of, as explained in the screenshot.

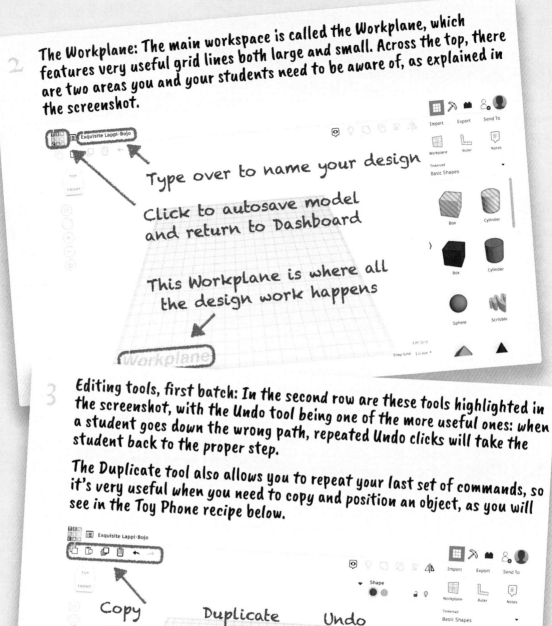

Type over to name your design

Click to autosave model and return to Dashboard

This Workplane is where all the design work happens

3   Editing tools, first batch: In the second row are these tools highlighted in the screenshot, with the Undo tool being one of the more useful ones: when a student goes down the wrong path, repeated Undo clicks will take the student back to the proper step.

The Duplicate tool also allows you to repeat your last set of commands, so it's very useful when you need to copy and position an object, as you will see in the Toy Phone recipe below.

Copy   Duplicate   Undo

Paste   Delete   Redo

4 Navigation tools: The column on the far left are the 3D Navigation tools to move in and around your designs. Ask your students to drag and drop any of the Basic Shapes on the right onto the Workplane and go through each navigation tool. For beginners, the View Cube is the most fun to use.

View Cube: for 360° view

Home: to reset your view
Fit view: zoom to selected item
Zoom in
Zoom out
Flat view: for budding engineers

5 Editing tools: On the top right hand side are tools to manipulate your models, where the Group tool is the most important while the Align tool is extremely useful. Use the Export icon to begin the 3D printing process. (Please see the Chapter Prepping a 3D Design for Printing.)

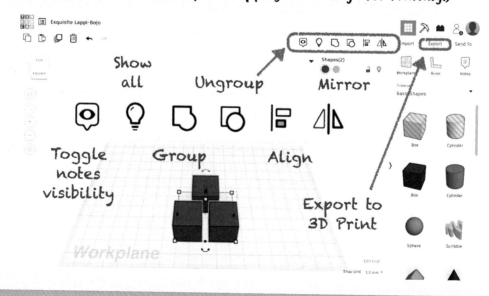

Show all

Ungroup

Mirror

Toggle notes visibility

Group

Align

Export to 3D Print

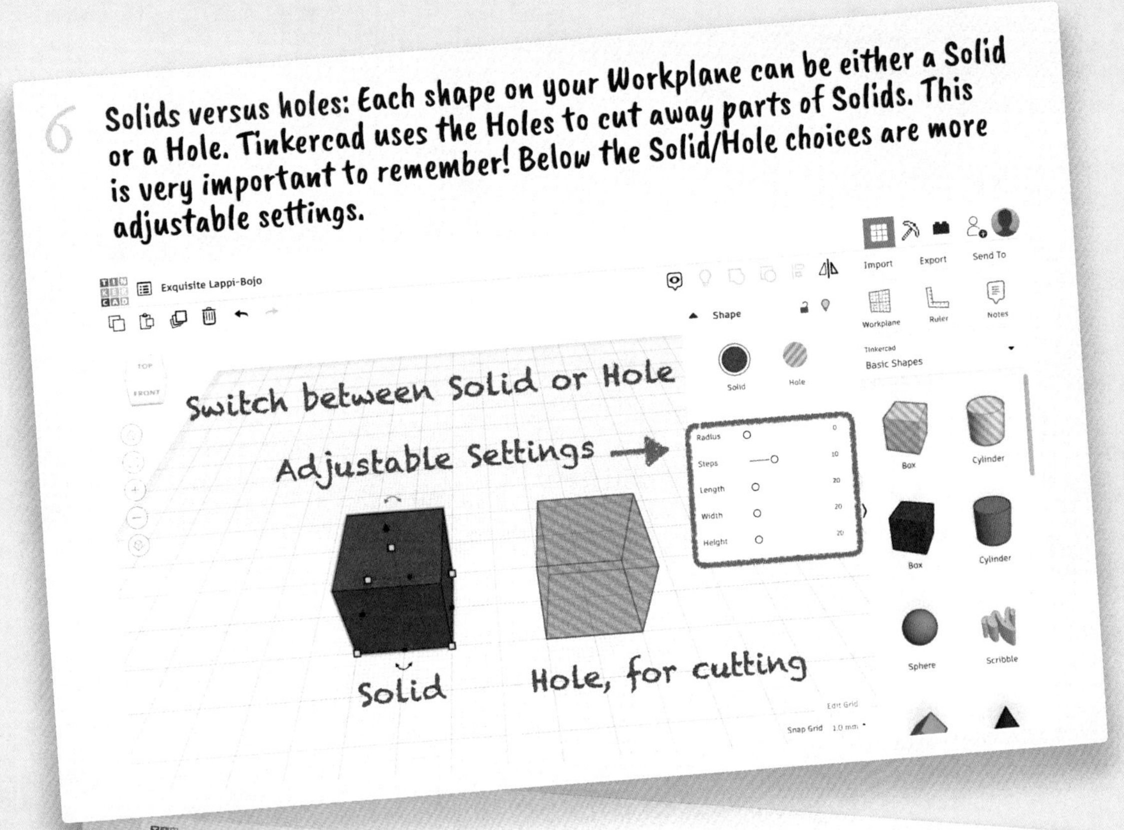
6
Solids versus holes: Each shape on your Workplane can be either a Solid or a Hole. Tinkercad uses the Holes to cut away parts of Solids. This is very important to remember! Below the Solid/Hole choices are more adjustable settings.
Exquisite Lappi-Bojo
Import
Export
Send To
Shape
Solid
Hole
Workplane
Ruler
Notes
Basic Shapes
Switch between Solid or Hole
Adjustable Settings
Radius
Steps
Length
Width
Height
Box
Cylinder
Sphere
Scribble
Solid
Hole, for cutting
Snap Grid

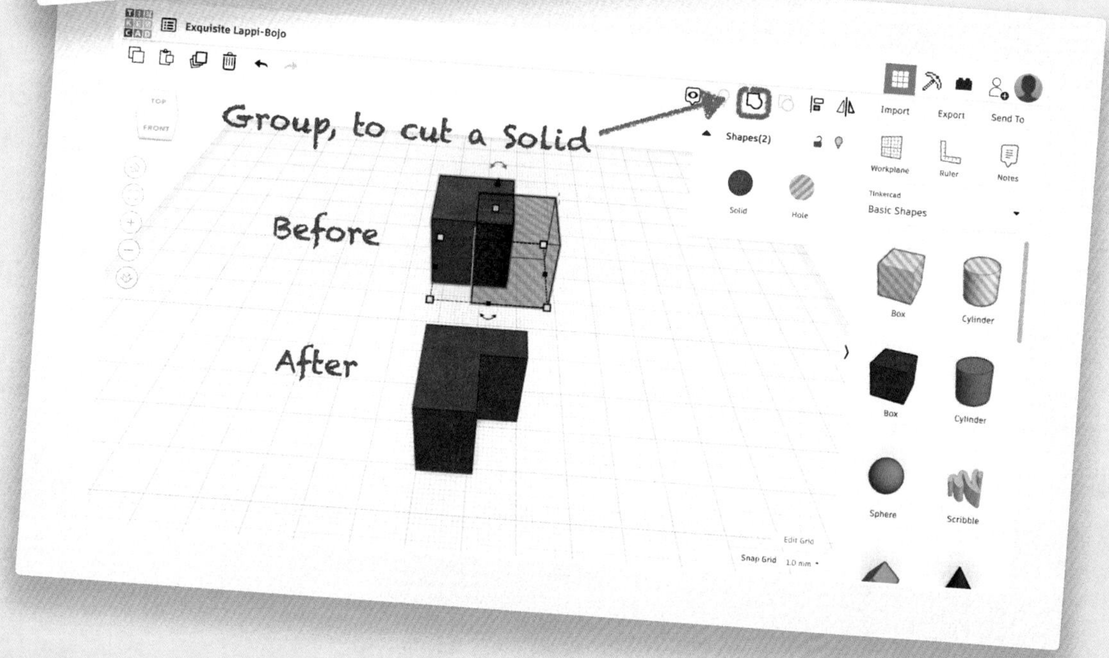
Exquisite Lappi-Bojo
Group, to cut a Solid
Import
Export
Send To
Shapes(2)
Solid
Hole
Workplane
Ruler
Notes
Basic Shapes
Before
After
Box
Cylinder
Sphere
Scribble
Snap Grid

7 Dropdown menus: The Car model below will show you how to use this very flexible Workplane tool while the Toy Phone will demonstrate the use of the Ruler. Below the Workplane and Ruler tools is a dropdown menu to a very wide array of choices, each with their own list of options. While this introductory book will focus mainly on the Basic Shapes, the children can explore and use these other options when they create their own models. There is a lot to choose from! If your students want to take a break from designing strictly in 3D, they can try the Scribble tool, which functions more like a 2D pen. Scribble is also useful when students want to create more organic shapes for their own designs.

Dropdown for other shapes and pre-made designs

Scribble, a 2D tool

8 Tools to change objects: Whenever you click any object on the Workplane, Tinkercad offers a wide number of choices allowing you to resize, reshape, or rotate your object. You can use your mouse to click and drag to move your object, but I've found that the arrow keys on your keyboard are far more exact. Another option is to just type in the amount that you want done. For example, you can type in "90" when you want to rotate your object by 90 degrees.

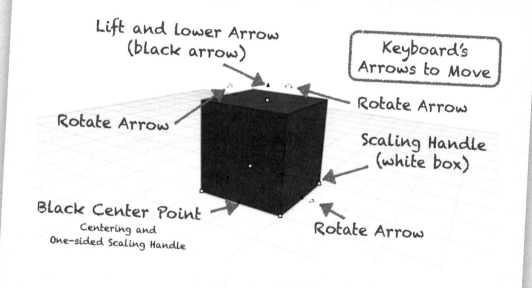

Lift and lower Arrow
(black arrow)

Keyboard's
Arrows to Move

Rotate Arrow

Rotate Arrow

Scaling Handle
(white box)

Black Center Point
Centering and
One-sided Scaling Handle

Rotate Arrow

Aleska Studio

NOWlab

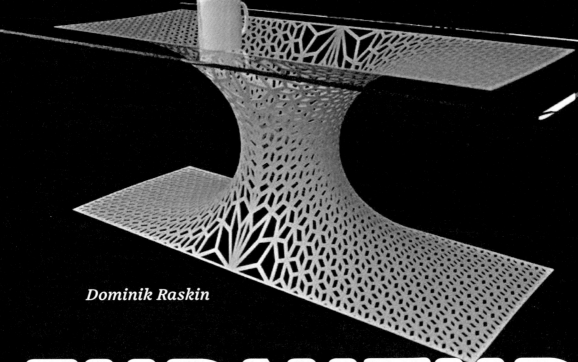

Dominik Raskin

FURNITURE

Mousarris Wave City

It's a curious fact:

The majority of the students (age 8-11) that I have encountered can't create this table on the first try: there are always one or more table legs that are misaligned.

It's okay.

It's the first model and it requires an exact use of the grids lines, emphasizing precision and accuracy.

Table

Box   Duplicate   Group   Handles   Lift and Lower

Workplane

1 Pick four large squares on the Workplane, these will help ensure your table legs are symmetrical with one another and positioned correctly later on. Just make sure you stay within those four large squares.

2 Place a Box inside the four squares.

3   Use a white Handle to modify the square to a 5x5 bottom in one corner of the four large squares —this will be the first table leg. In this example, the leg is in the lower left hand corner of the four squares.

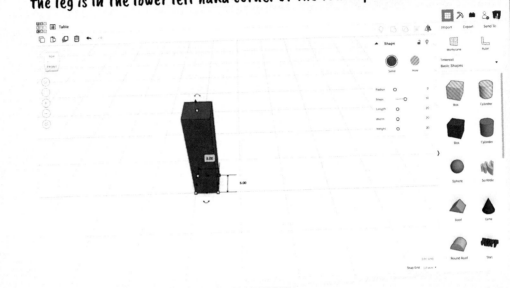

4   Duplicate the table leg once using the Duplicate tool in the upper left hand corner. (The duplicate will occupy the same place as the original)

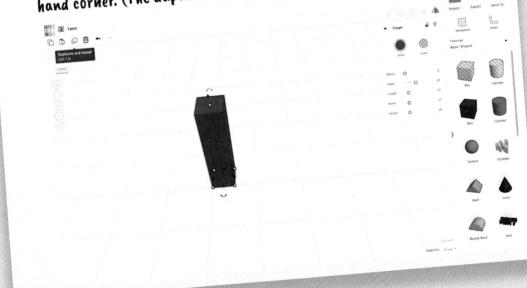

5 Move the duplicate to the other side of the four large squares, staying within the original four large squares on the Workplane.

6 Using your cursor, click and drag across both table legs to select both legs.

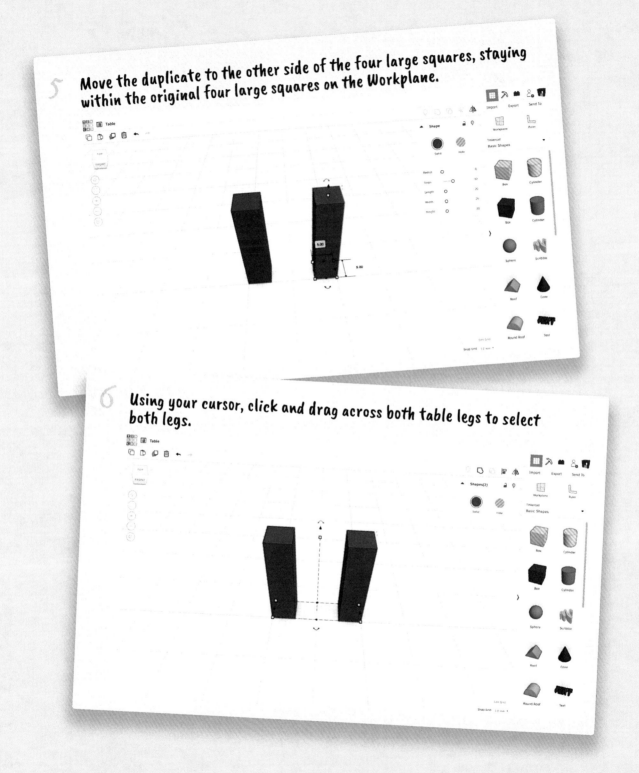

7 Duplicate both table legs, again with the Duplicate tool.

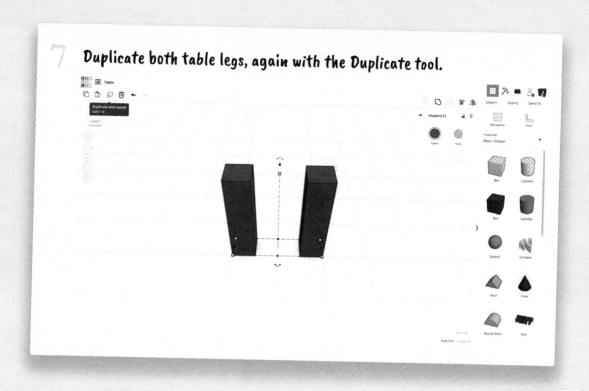

8 Move both duplicates to the other side of the four large squares. Here, they are at the back of the originally selected four large squares.

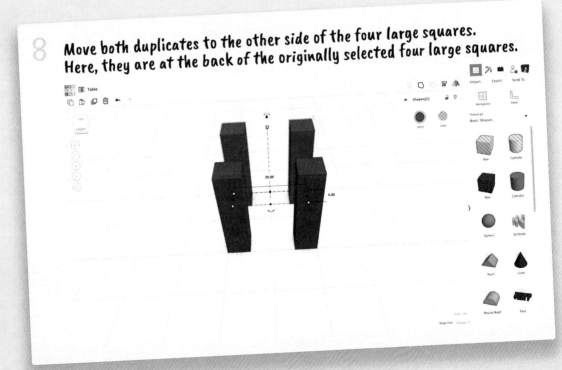

9 Place a new red solid Box inside the original four large squares. This will initially cover the four table legs you have already created.

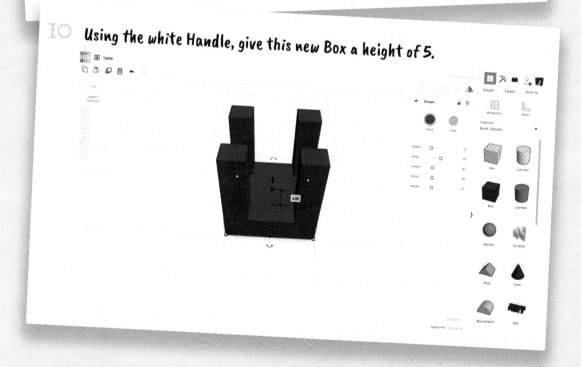

10 Using the white Handle, give this new Box a height of 5.

II Use the black lift arrow tool to lift the table top by 15 to the top of the table legs.

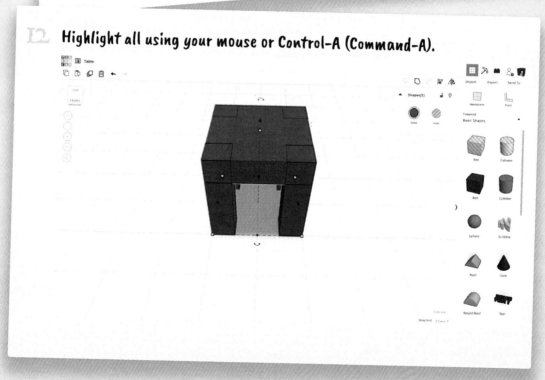

I2 Highlight all using your mouse or Control-A (Command-A).

13 Group all with the Group tool on the upper right hand editing tools.

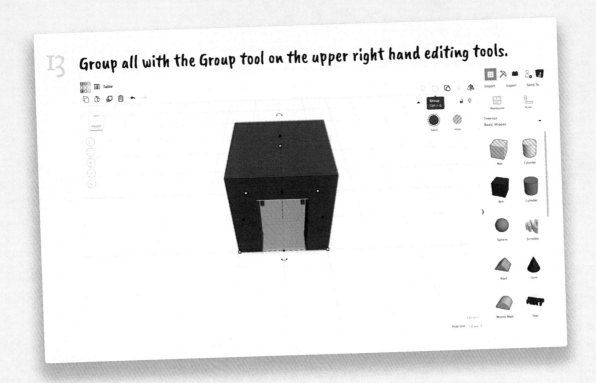

14 Done!

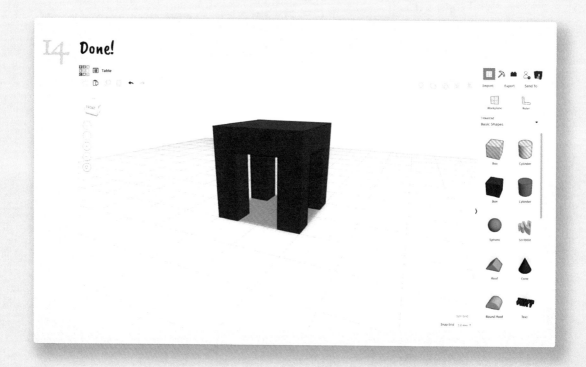

ClosetMaid 2-Tier Square Wood Side Table with Storage Shelf

VASAGLE eettafel voor 4 personen via VLAKKO.nl

CHALLENGE!

Kennedy dining table by FocusOn Furniture & Bedding

Daniel Christian Tang

Fathom & Form

JEWELRY

The crux of this model is the step rotating the Roof from a horizontal to virtual position.

You need to get a side view to do this or the Rotate tool is hidden from view.

Ring

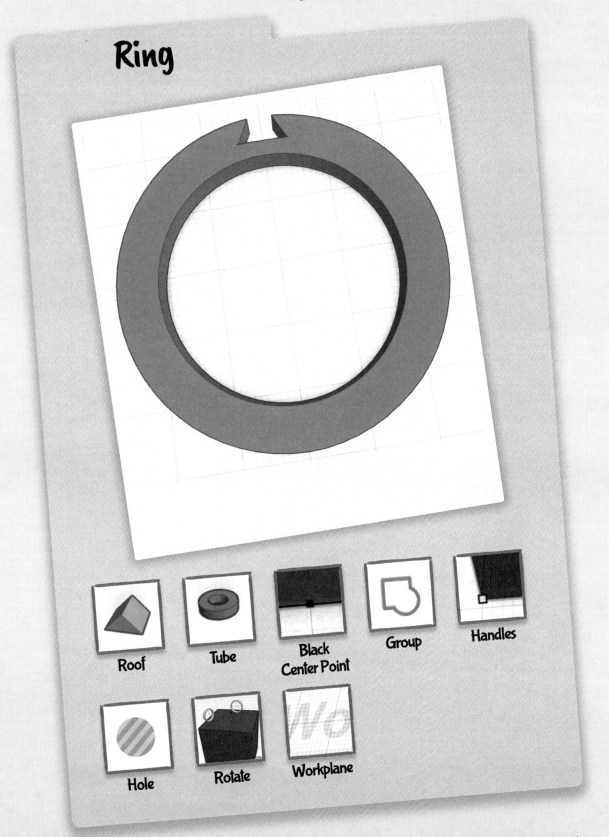

Roof

Tube

Black
Center Point

Group

Handles

Hole

Rotate

Workplane

Under Basic Shapes, put a Tube on the Workplane.

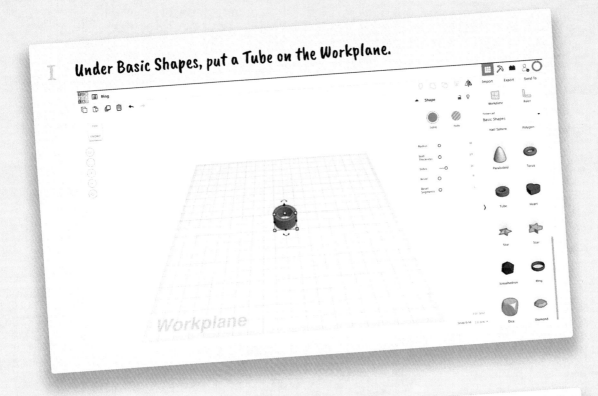

Make it 50x50x5 by just typing over the dimension numbers.

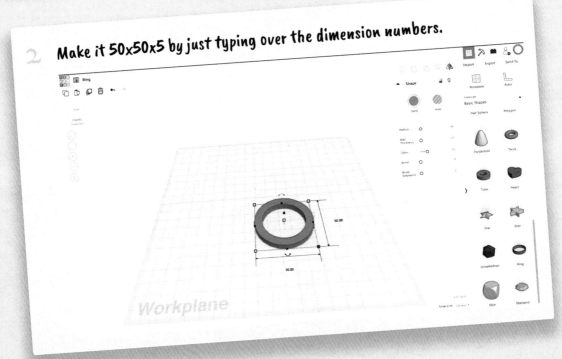

3 Increase Sides to 64 to make it smoother.

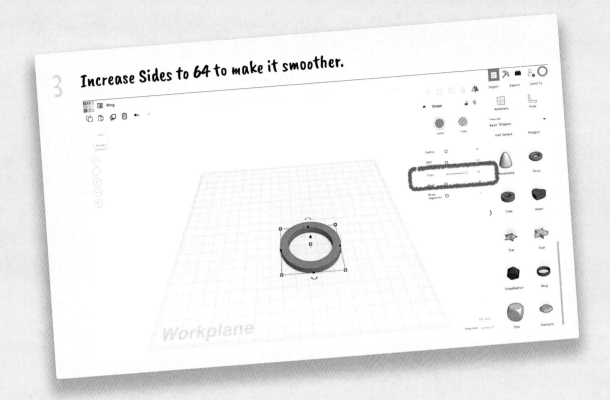

4 Put a Roof on the Workplane.

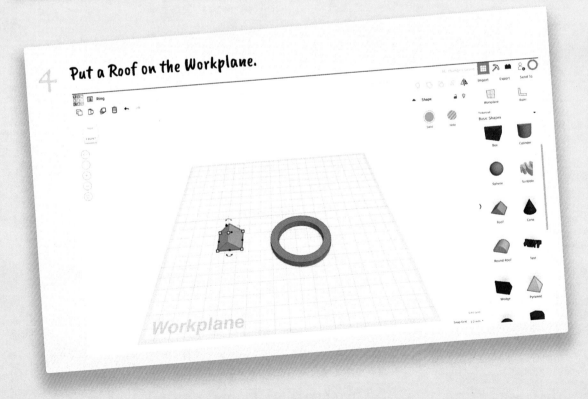

5 After using the View Cube to orbit and view from a side angle, rotate the Roof 90 degrees to an upright position, with the roof top facing the back and the base of the Roof facing the front.

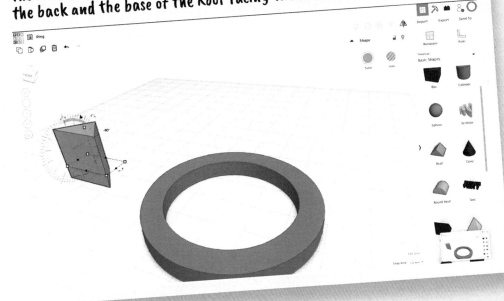

6 Make the Roof's bottom 8x8.

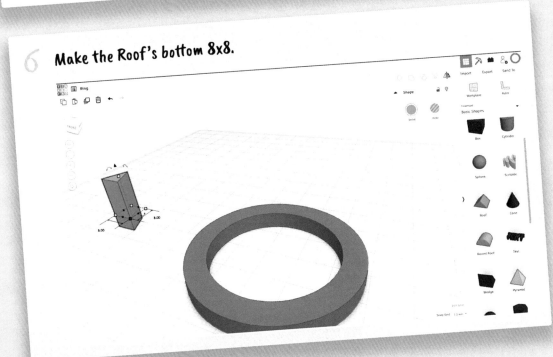

7 Move the Roof to the top of the Tube, lining up their Black Center Points.

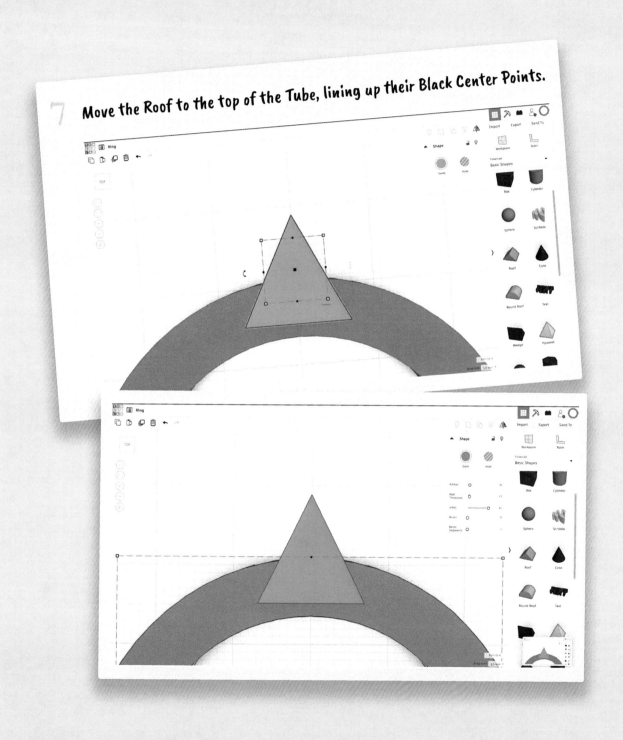

8   Change the Roof from a Solid into a Hole.

9   Highlight the roof and the ring.

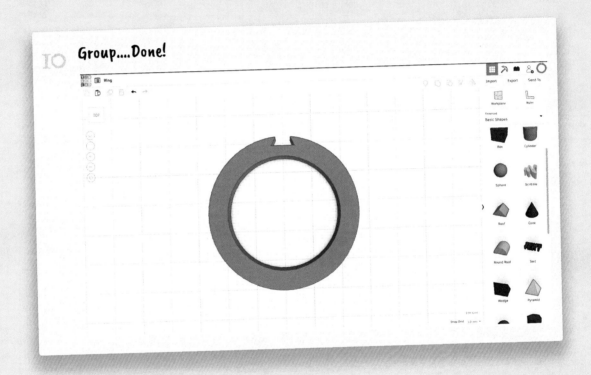

David Seto & Michael Welch

CHALLENGE!

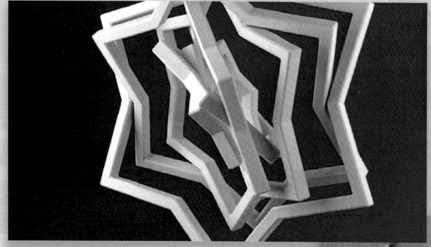

New Story

The Infinity 3D Crane Wasp Printer

Houben/Van Mierlo Architects

ARCHITECTURE

Dubai 3D Printing Strategy

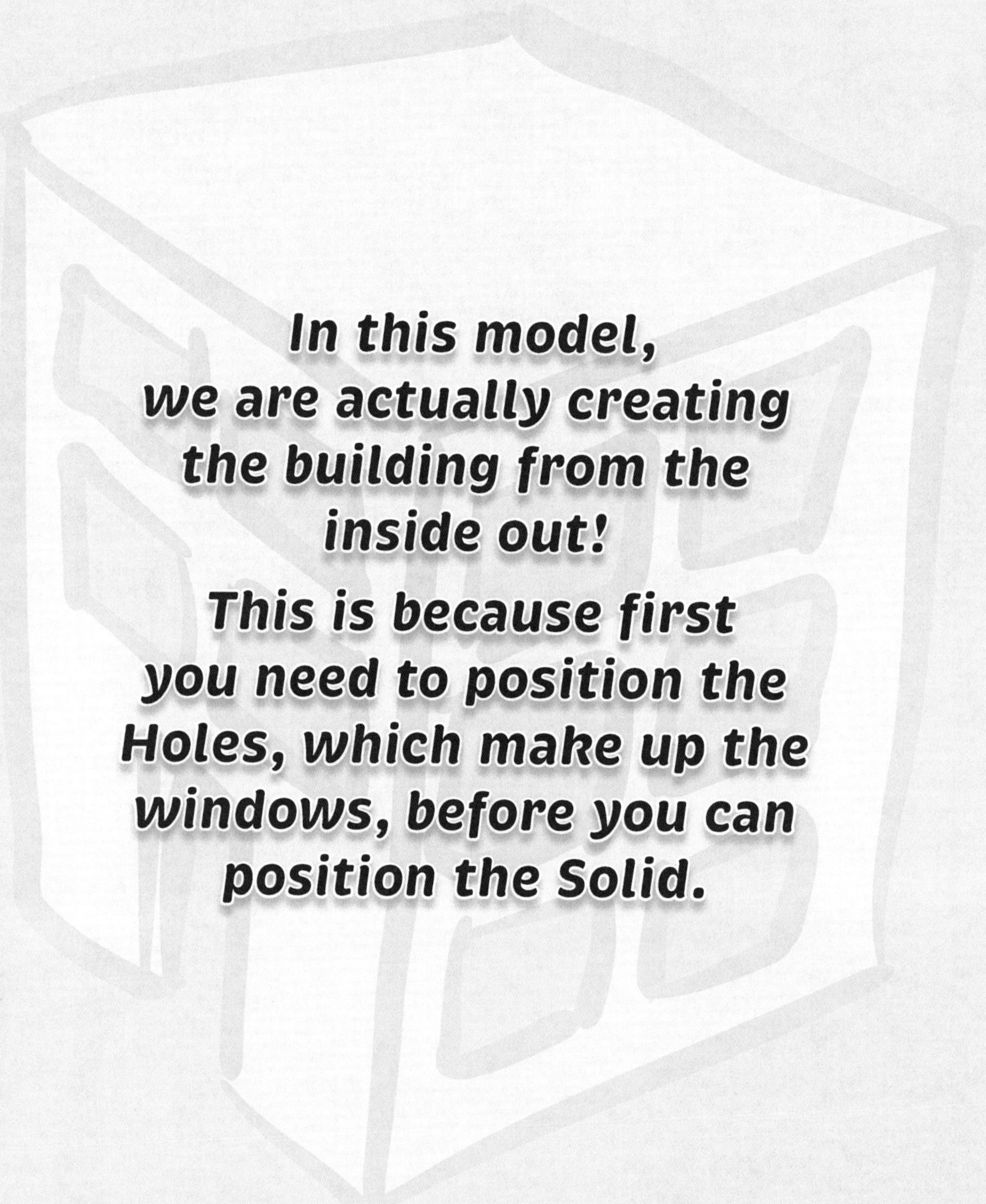

**In this model,
we are actually creating
the building from the
inside out!**

**This is because first
you need to position the
Holes, which make up the
windows, before you can
position the Solid.**

Building

Box

Box
(Hole)

Duplicate

Group

Handles

Lift and
Lower

Workplane

1. Pick four large squares on the Workplane; note the center line. Everything needs to stay inside these four squares.

2. Place a Box Hole inside the four squares.

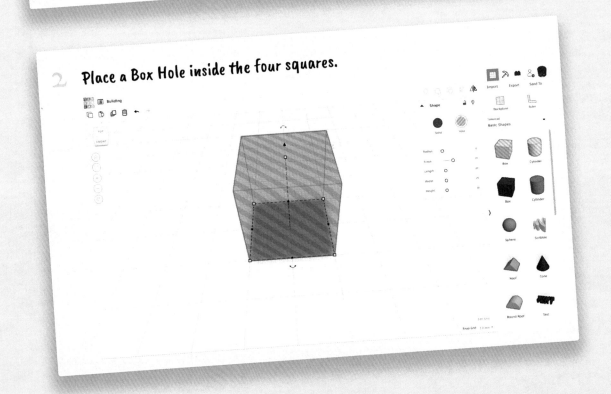

3 Click the upper-right corner Handle, holding down Shift, and make a 5x5x5 box at the bottom left corner of the four large squares. When you hold down the Shift key, all three dimensions scale uniformly.

4 Slide the Box Hole to two small squares to the left of the center line.

Center Line

Two small squares

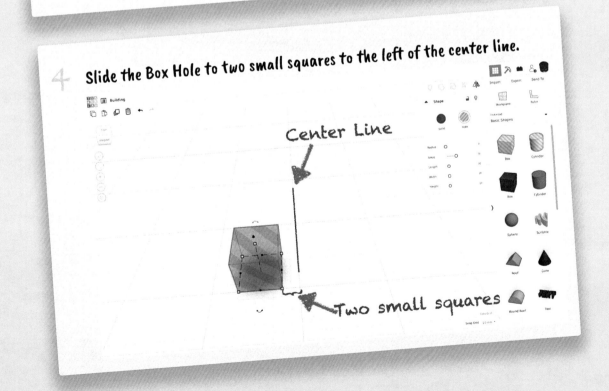

5 Duplicate the Box Hole. (Again, it'll appear over the original Box Hole)

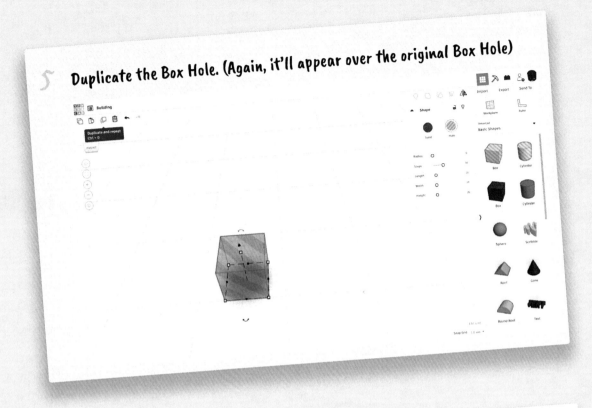

6 Move the duplicate Box Hole two small squares to the right of the center line.

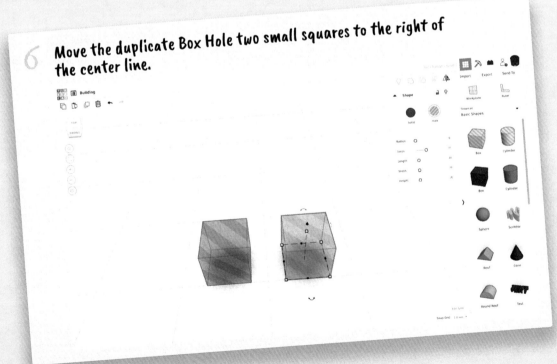

7 Highlight both Box Holes.

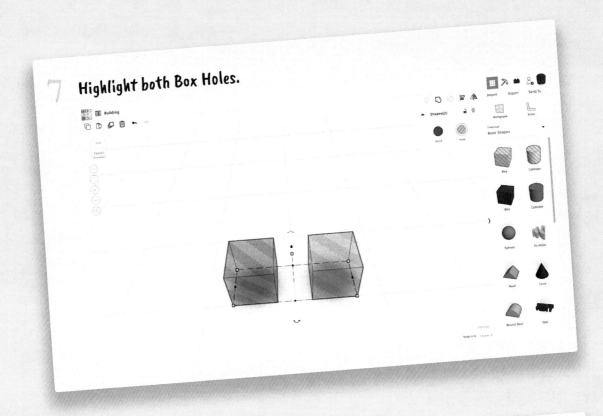

8 Use the Lift Arrow to lift the Box Holes in the air to 10.

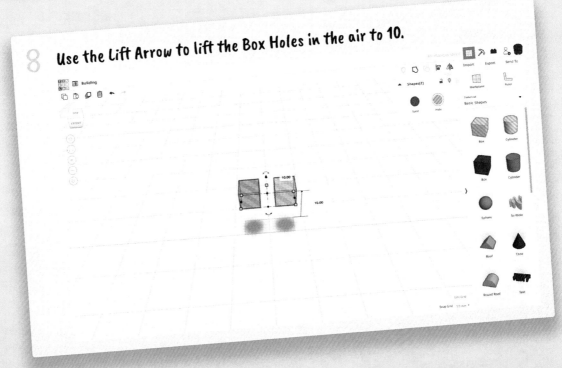

9 Duplicate the pair of Box Holes again.

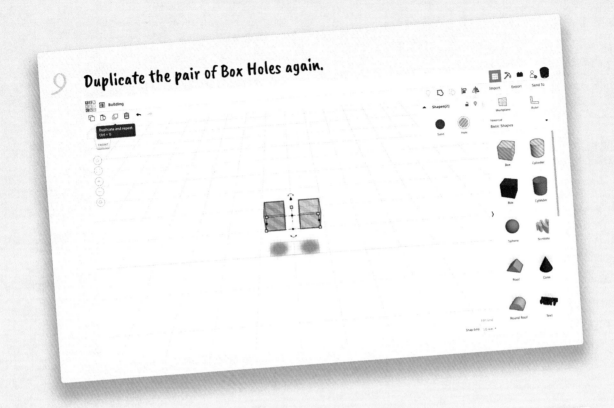

10 Use the Lift Arrow to lift the new duplicate set up to 20.

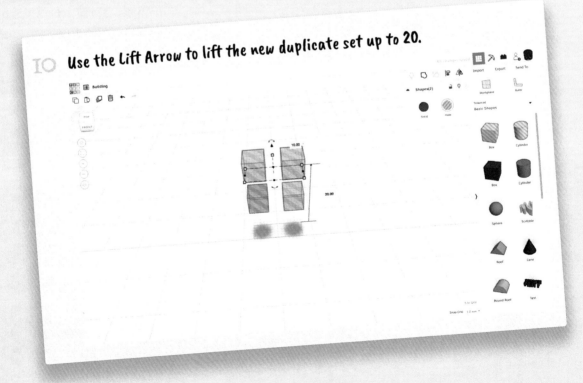

11 Place another Box Hole inside the original four squares.

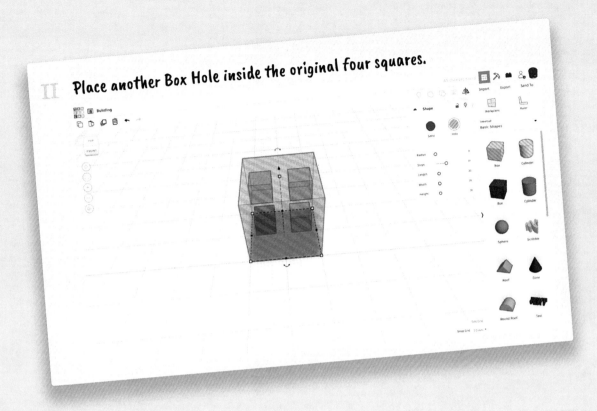

12 Use a Handle, hold down Shift, and make a 6x6x6 box for the door.

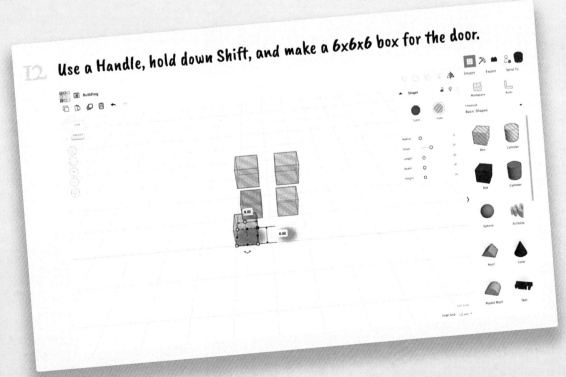

13 Line up the door squarely on the center line.

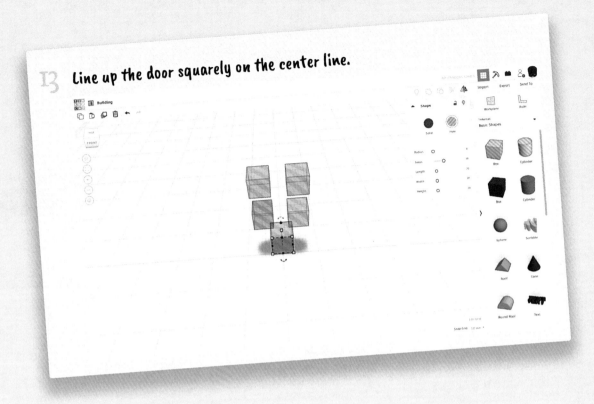

14 Place another Box Hole inside the four squares.

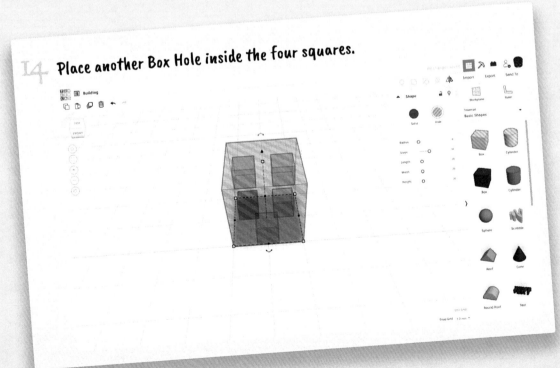

15 Use a Handle to change the bottom to 18x18.

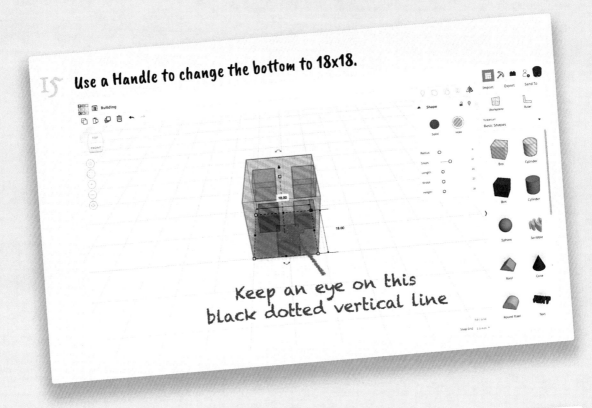

Keep an eye on this
black dotted vertical line

16 Place this large box at the center of four squares; use the black dotted
vertical line in the middle.

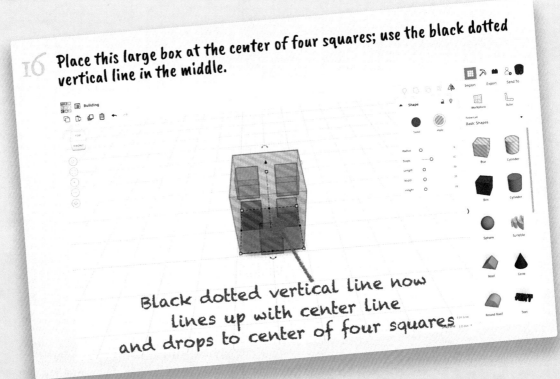

Black dotted vertical line now
lines up with center line
and drops to center of four squares

17 Make the height of this Box Hole 28.

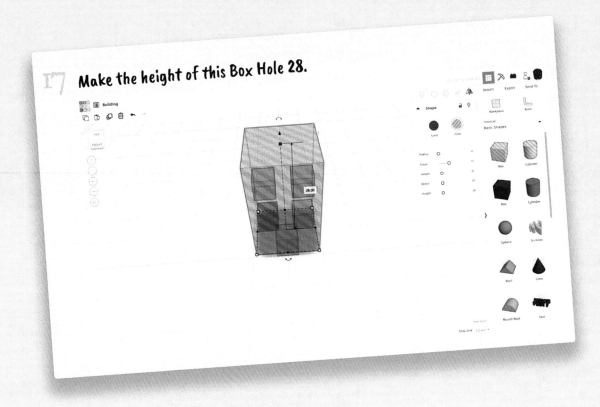

18 Place a solid Box inside the four squares.

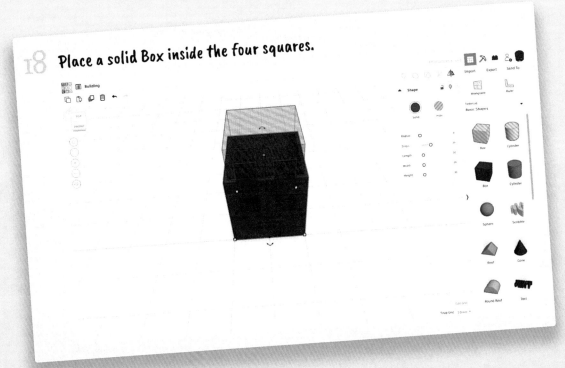

19 **Give Box a height of 30.**

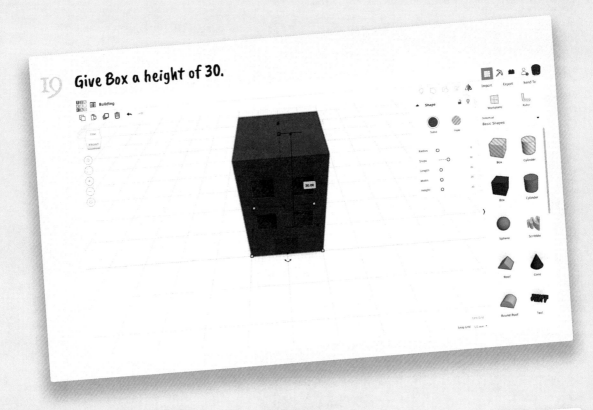

20 **Highlight all and then Group....**

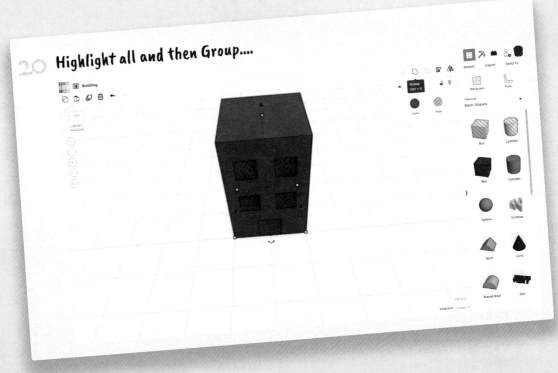

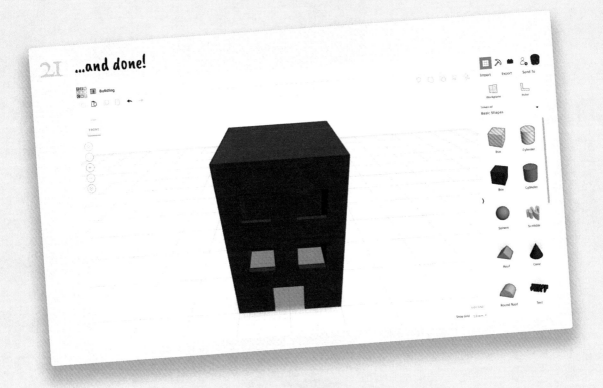

The Hive, Singapore

CHALLENGE!

Burj Khalifa by Picslover via Zedge

The De Rotterdam complex by Ryan Koopman / Getty Images

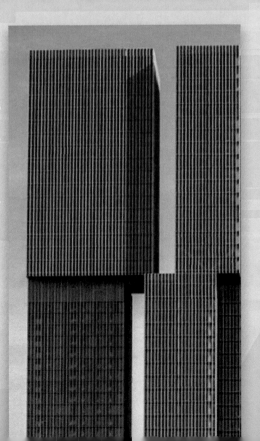

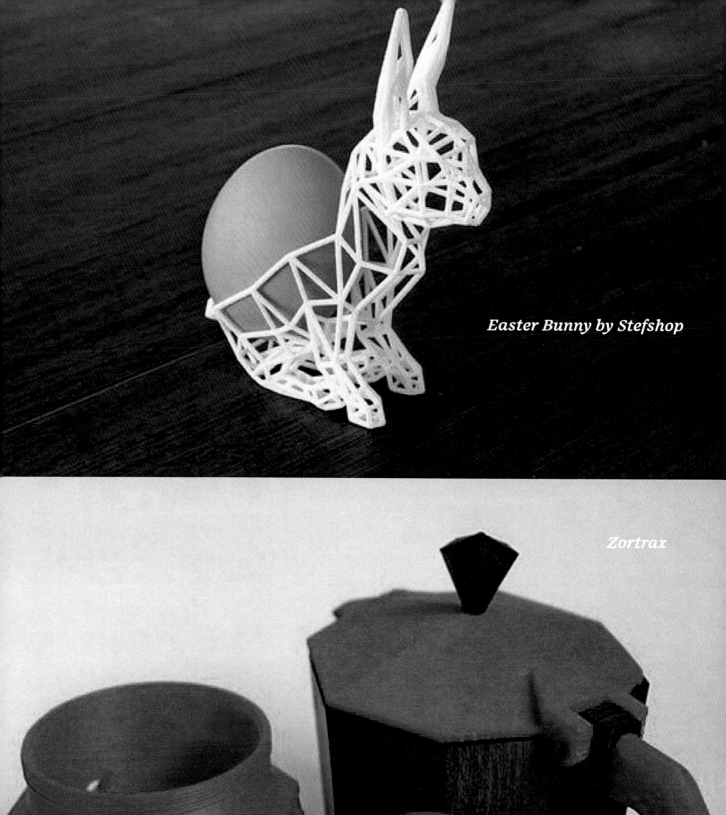

Easter Bunny by Stefshop

Zortrax

KITCHEN

Francis Bitonti".

Joe Doucet

Make sure the students stay within the four squares on the Workplane or the cup will be lopsided.

Cup

Cone   Paraboloid   Group   Handles   Hole

Lift and Lower   Rotate   Workplane

1 Pick four large squares on the Workplane, again noting the center line.

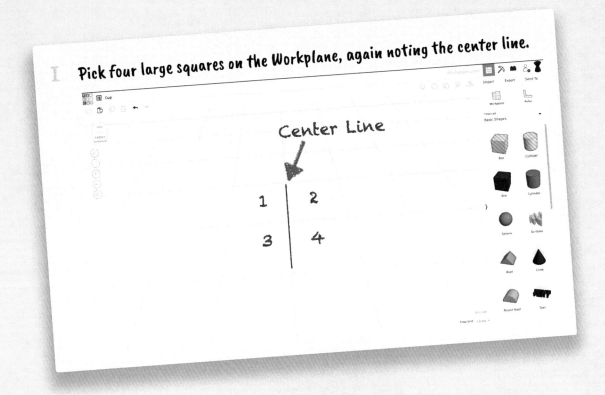

2 Place a Cone inside the four squares, then increase Sides to smooth it.

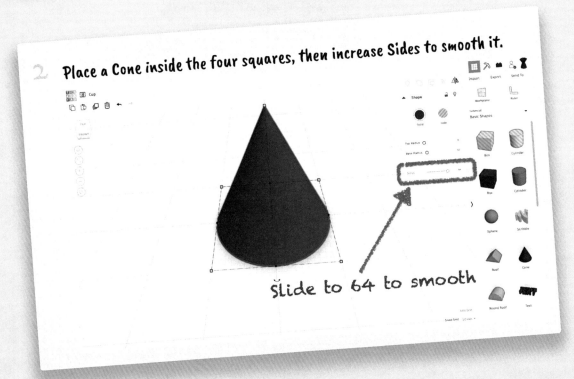

3 Hold down shift and drag any Handle to make the cone 18x18x18.

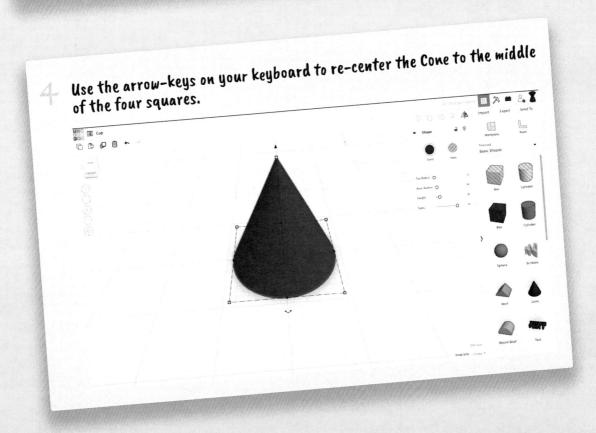

4 Use the arrow-keys on your keyboard to re-center the Cone to the middle of the four squares.

5 **Click Hole to turn the Cone into a hole.**

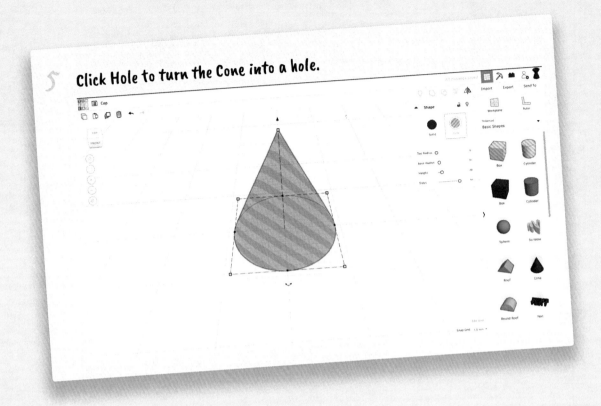

6 **Place a new Cone on top of the Cone Hole and increase its Sides to smooth the shape of the Cone.**

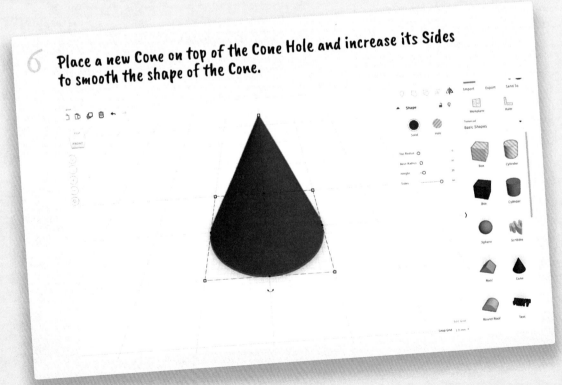

7   Highlight both and Group. Though you can't see it because it's covered, when you Group a Solid with a Hole, the Hole cuts away any part of the Solid that overlaps with the Hole.

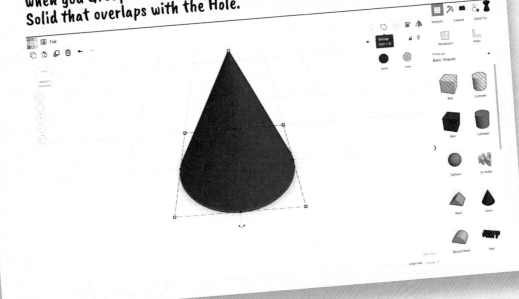

8   Rotate the object 180 degrees so you can see that the Hole has cut away part of the Solid.

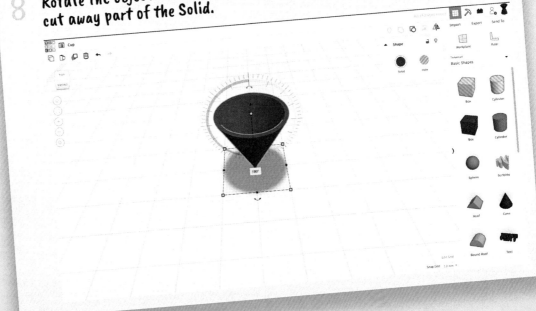

9   **Lift the hollowed Cone up 10.**

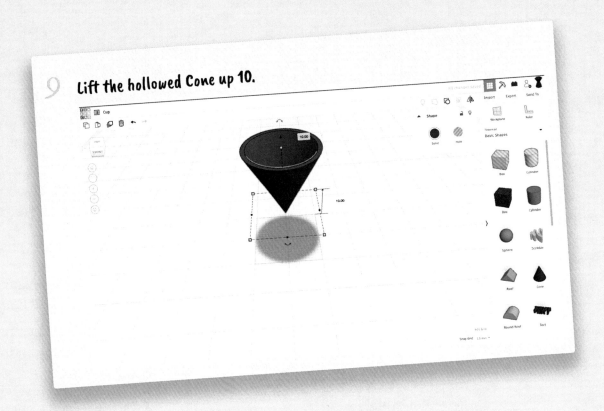

IO   **Place a Paraboloid in the center of the four large squares.**

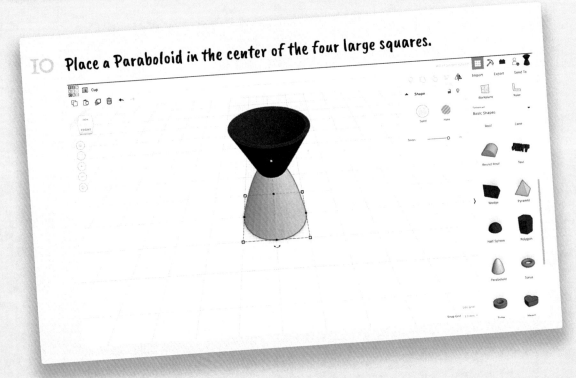

II Highlight the Paraboloid and the Cone.

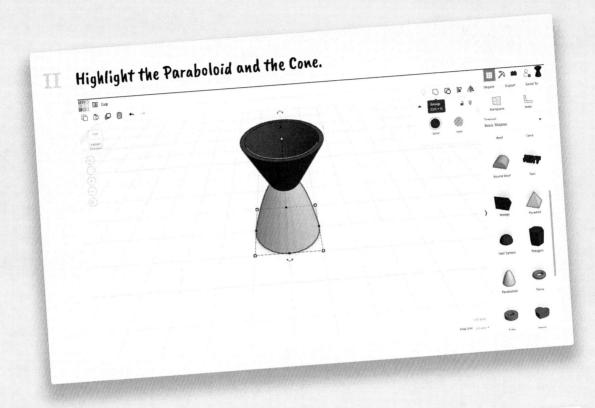

12 Group....Done!

David Seto & Michael Welch

Blue Solo Cup 16 oz.

CHALLENGE!

Basketball Mug with Hoop
via totsfamily.com

BEEVERYCREATIVE

Pip Boxes by Andrew Askedall

Drills

Plantygons by Printfutura

DECOR

R4 Retro Clock by Nemor

This is an all time favorite for many of the younger students because they can easily customize it.

But this model introduces the very important Align tool which makes lining up two objects extremely easy.

Heart-shaped Box

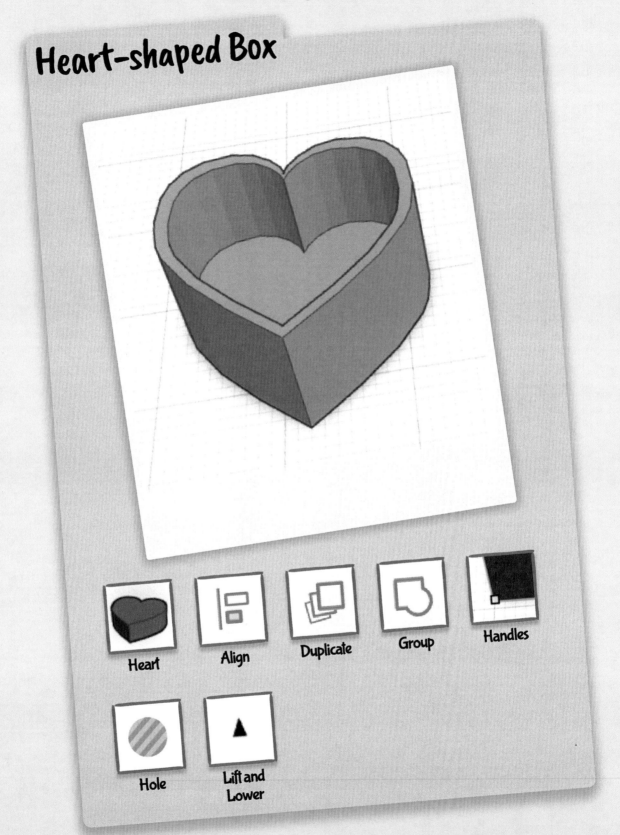

Heart   Align   Duplicate   Group   Handles

Hole   Lift and Lower

1 Under Basic Shapes, put a Heart on the Workplane.

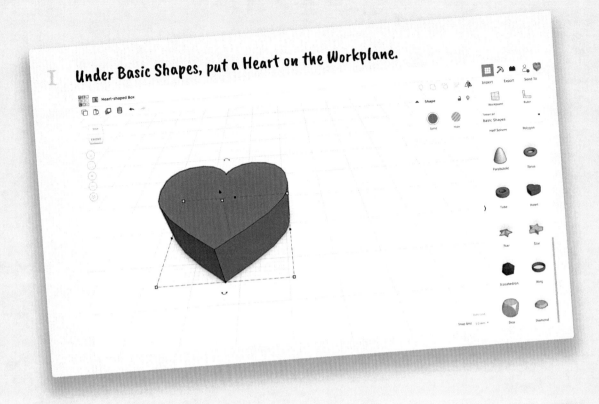

2 Make it 20x20x3 where the 3 is the height.

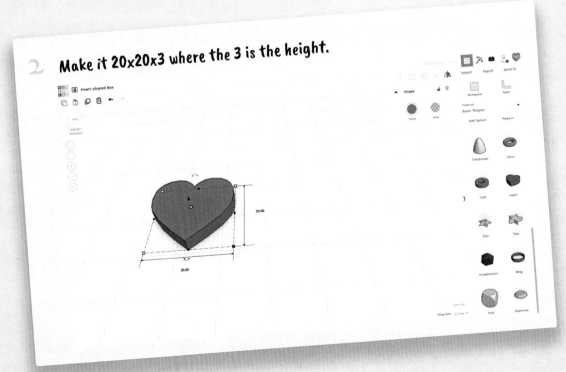

3 Duplicate it and move this first duplicate to one side. This duplicate will later be used to create the lid for the box.

4 Return to the first Heart and increase its height to 10.

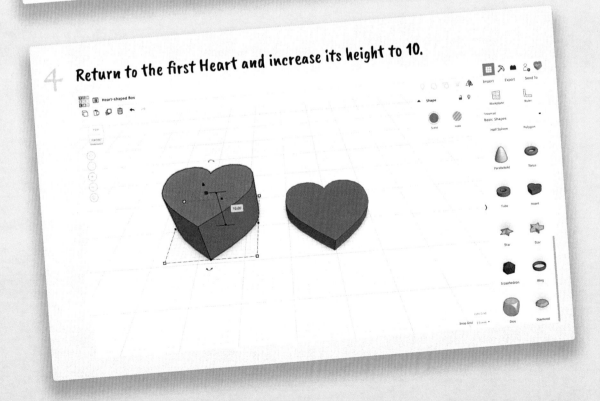

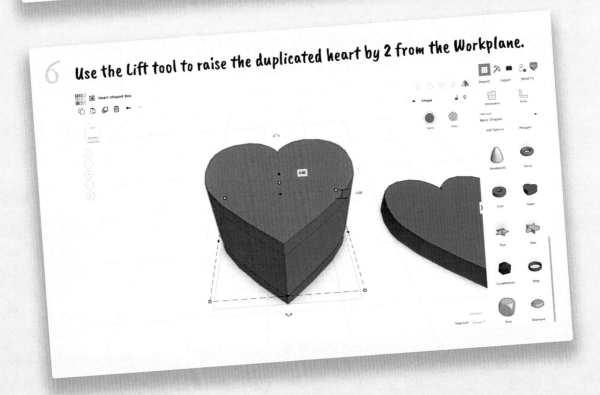

5 Now, Duplicate this heart again to make your second duplicate, which we will later use for hollowing out the heart-shaped box.

6 Use the Lift tool to raise the duplicated heart by 2 from the Workplane.

7 **Use the Handle of the Duplicate heart and make it 18x18 on the bottom.**

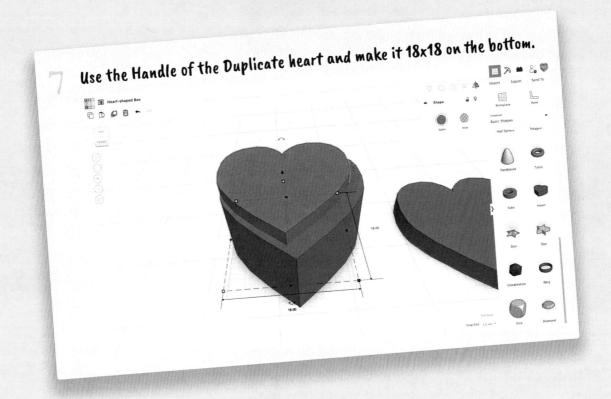

8 **Highlight both the top and bottom Hearts and click the Align tool on the upper right hand of the screen. The Align tool is a very important and useful tool!**

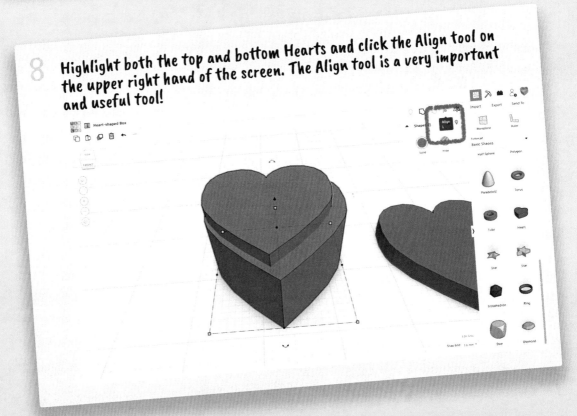

9   Click the black dots on the side and bottom center to align along those two directions. After you click them, the black dots turn gray to signal the alignment is done. Click anywhere on the Workplane to exit the Align tool.

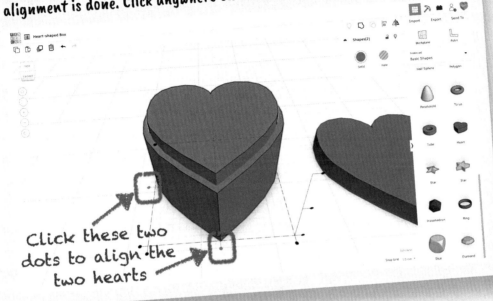

Click these two dots to align the two hearts

10   Now we can make the duplicated Heart on top into a Hole (or cutout) of the heart-shaped box.

Highlight the top and bottom Hearts and Group.

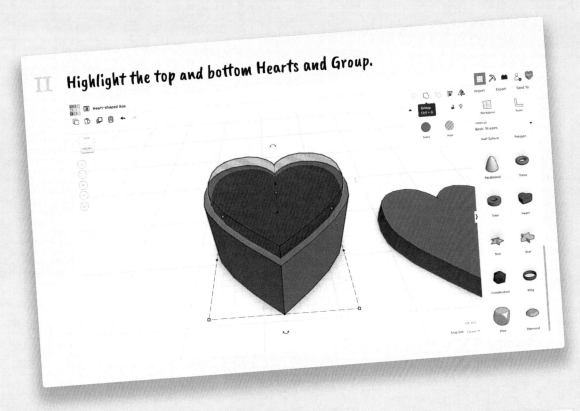

When you Group a Solid with a Hole, the Hole cuts away part of the Solid.

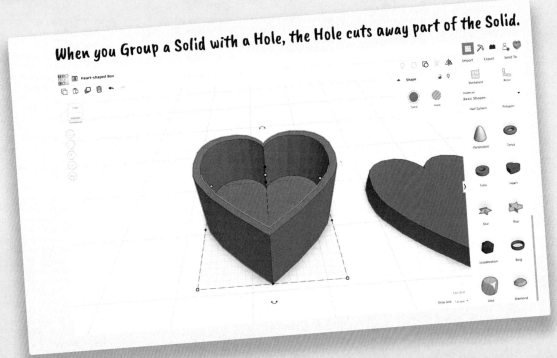

12 Go to the other Heart on the side to begin making the lid.

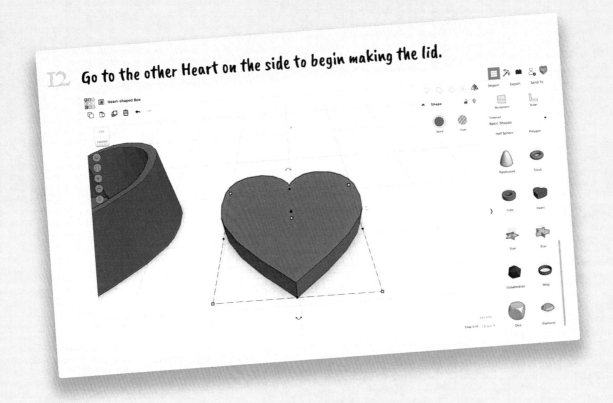

13 Duplicate and raise the duplicate by 1 from the Workplane.

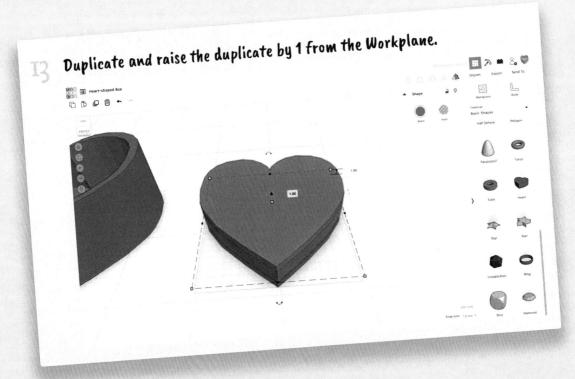

14 Give the duplicate a size of 17.8x17.8 along the bottom. This extrusion will prevent the lid from sliding off the box.

15 Highlight the top and bottom Heart and click the Align tool.

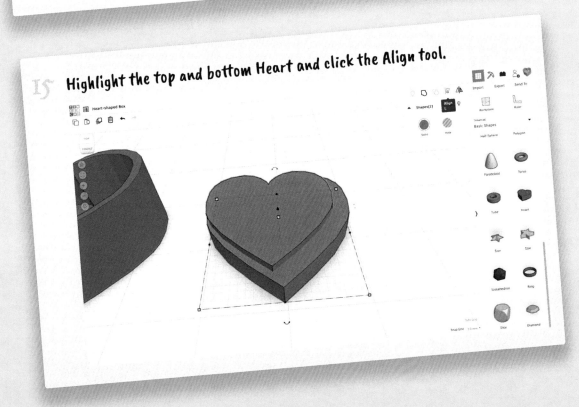

16 Center Align the front and the side, then click anywhere on Workplane.

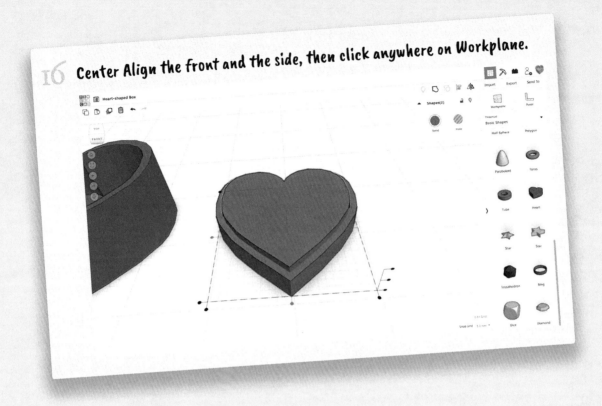

17 Highlight both parts of the lid and Group them together.

Click to change color

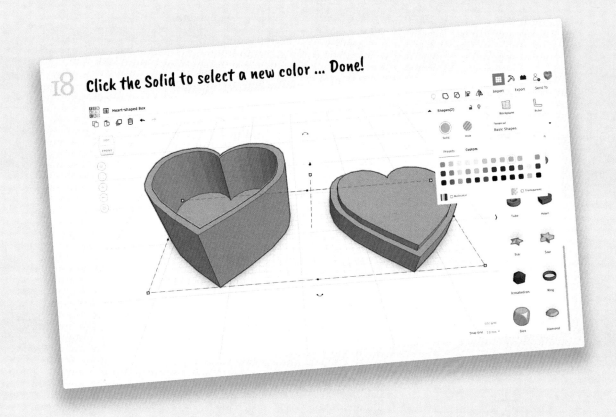

Z GALLERIE INSPIRED DECORATIVE BOXES
from Studio 36 interiors

CHALLENGE!

*Everly QUINN Lappin 2 Piece Snake Print
Decorative Box Set VIA WAYFAIR*

*Pavilion Chic Decorative Boxes Art Deco Style
by Pavilion Broadway*

Windup Motor by BRICO3D

TINY CAR CARRIER by agep.biz

3D Systems's Cubify Robots

TOYS

The XR-35 by Blokko's Prad La

This model introduces how to use the Ruler and Repeat tools. The Ruler lets you see all the dimensions of all the objects simultaneously which is handy when your Workplane gets a bit crowded. The Repeat Tool, which is just the Duplicate Tool used repeatedly, is a massive time saver. Just make sure you don't click anything else before you start the repeat sequence. Otherwise, the mouse clicks you want to duplicate are canceled.

Toy Phone

Box

Box
(Hole)

Duplicate

Group

Handles

Lift and
Lower

Ruler

Workplane

1 Place a Ruler on the Workplane where two heavy lines meet.

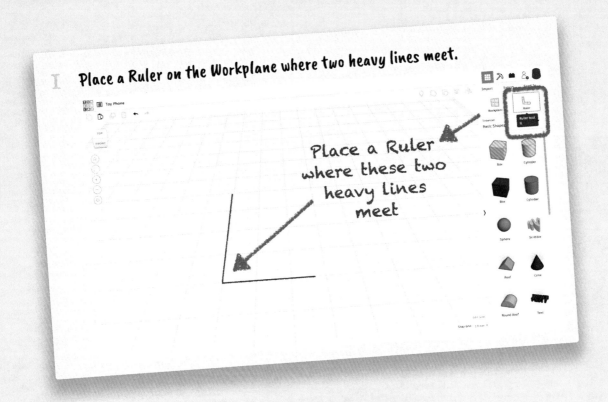

Place a Ruler where these two heavy lines meet

2 Make sure you have enough space on the Workplane on the upper right.

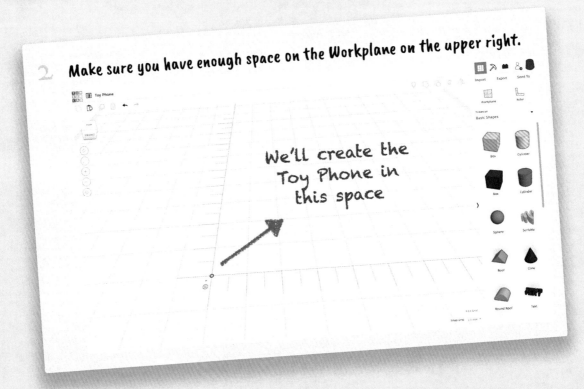

We'll create the Toy Phone in this space

3 Place a solid Box where its lower left corner meets the Ruler's Origin.

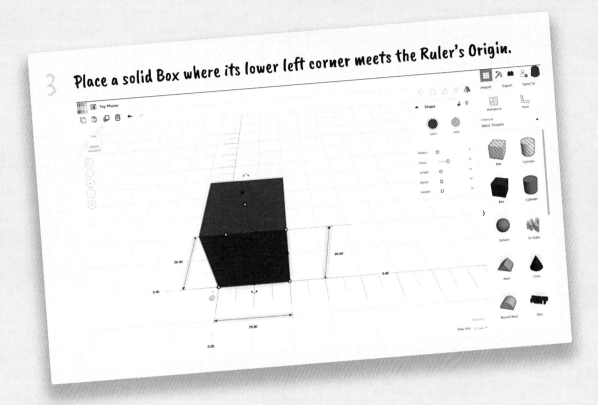

4. Holding down the Shift key, click the upper right Handle and pull it inwards to make the Box 5x5x5.

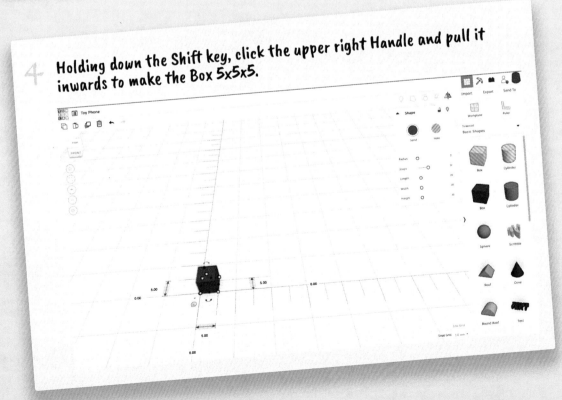

5 Duplicate the Box.

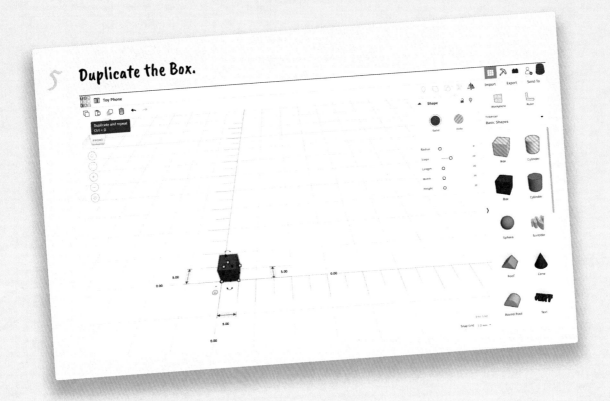

6 Use the Right Arrow key on your keyboard to slide the Box to the right by 10 small squares.

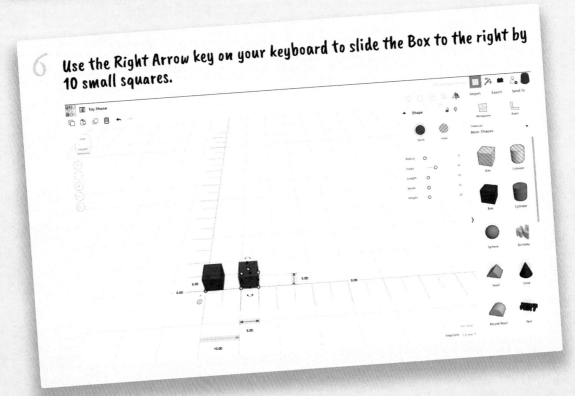

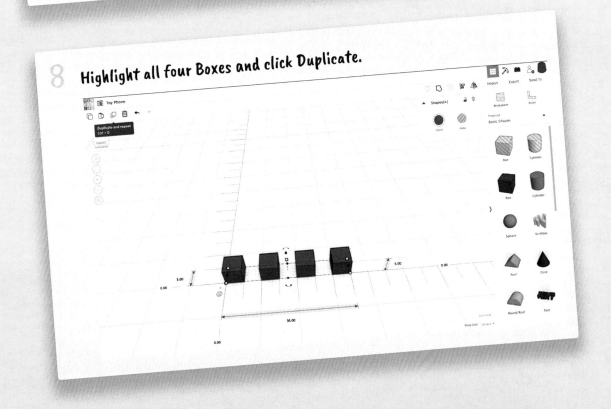

7 Click Duplicate two more times to create two more Boxes on the right. This is the very useful Repeat tool in Tinkercad!

8 Highlight all four Boxes and click Duplicate.

9　Use the Up Arrow Key on your keyboard to slide the four Boxes up by 10 small squares.

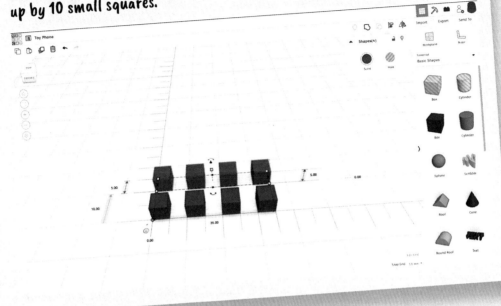

10　Click Duplicate two more times for a total of 16 Boxes.

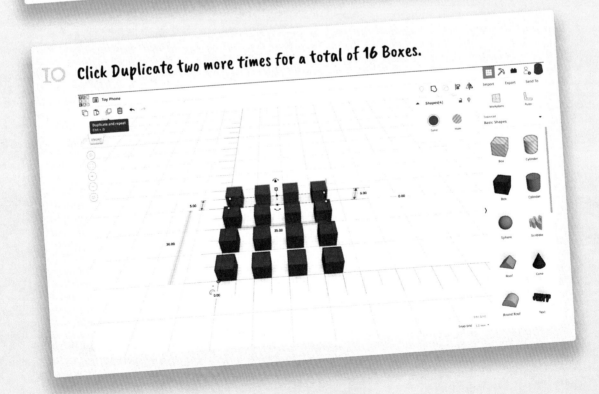

II Orbit and place a Box Hole along the first heavy line above the **16 Boxes**.

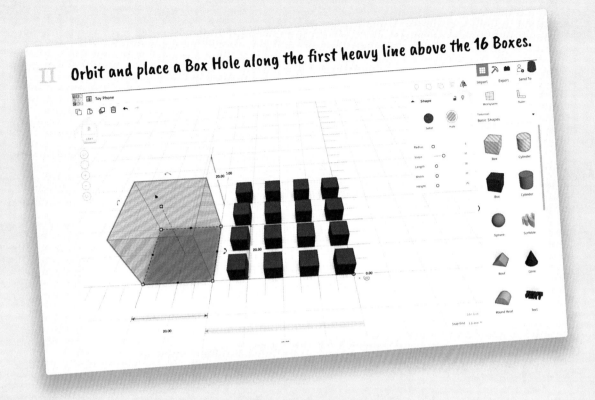

I2 Make the Box Hole **35x20** on its bottom.

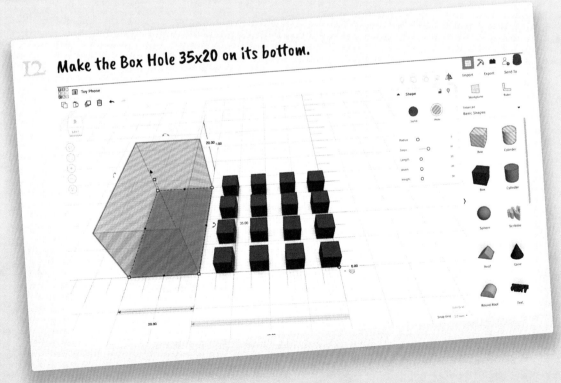

13 **Orbit again, use the Lift tool to raise the Box Hole height to 2.**

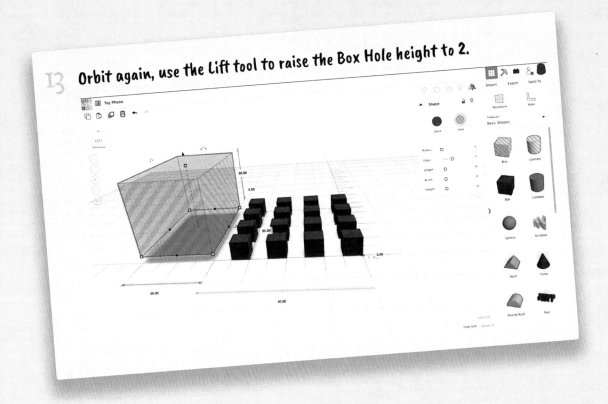

14 **Move the Ruler's Origin point left by 5 small squares and then down by another 5 small squares on the Workplane. The Origin will end up in the middle of a large square.**

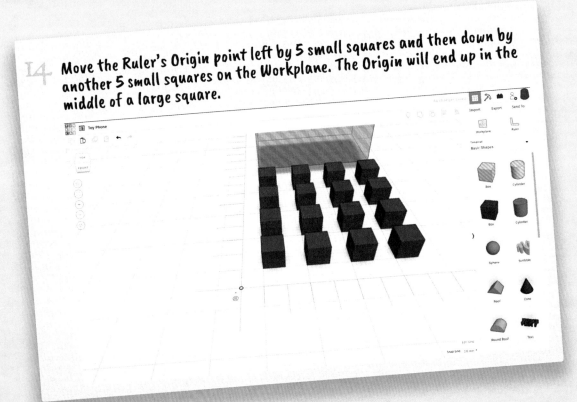

15 **Place a solid Box where its lower left corner meets the Ruler's new Origin.**

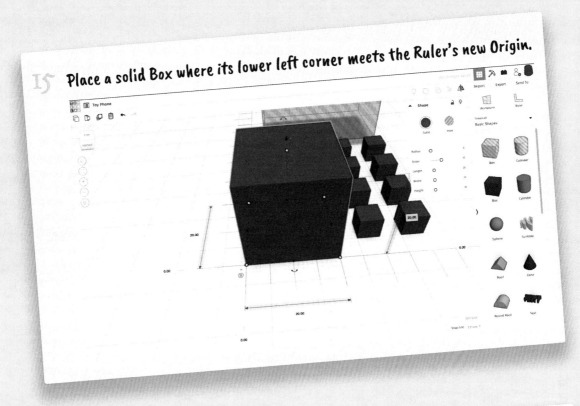

16 **Make the Box 70x45x4 and dismiss the Ruler.**

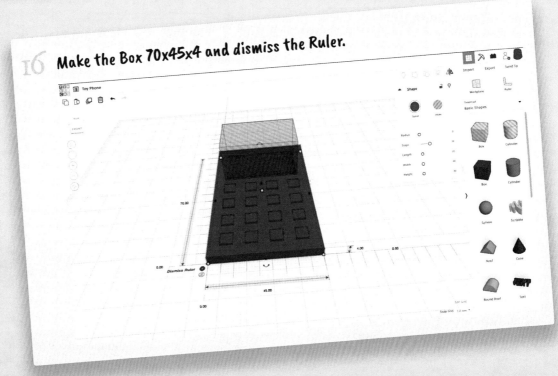

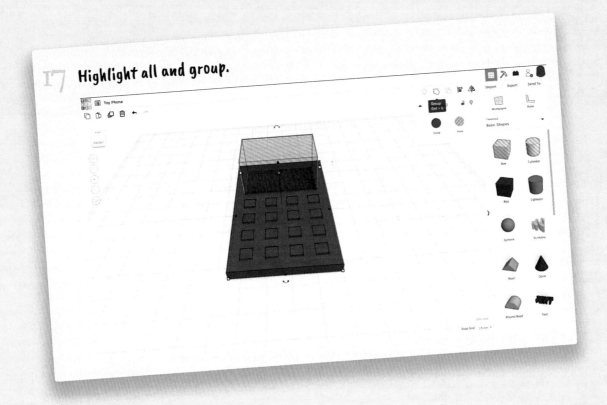

17 Highlight all and group.

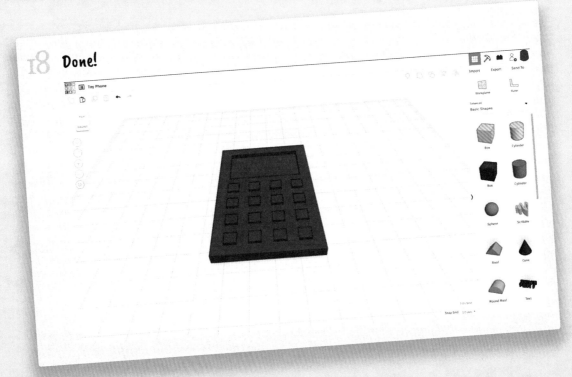

18 Done!

Anytech SUP 400 in 1 Games Retro Game Box Console Handheld

CHALLENGE!

Handheld Raspberry Pi Video Game Console Retro CM3 Mini Pocket Player via AliExpress

Upprinting Food

ChefJet Candy

Choc Edge.

Dinara Kasko

This model introduces the Text tool which allows students to customize their own future models with words of their own choosing.

But please, anything else but more name tags!

Chocolate Bar

Box

Box
(Hole)

Text

Align

Group

Handles

Lift and
Lower

Ruler

1 Place a Ruler anywhere on the Workplane. Unlike the Toy Phone, the Chocolate Bar does not need exact positioning because we'll be using the Align tool to position the parts.

2 Place a Box anywhere and make it 40x20x4.

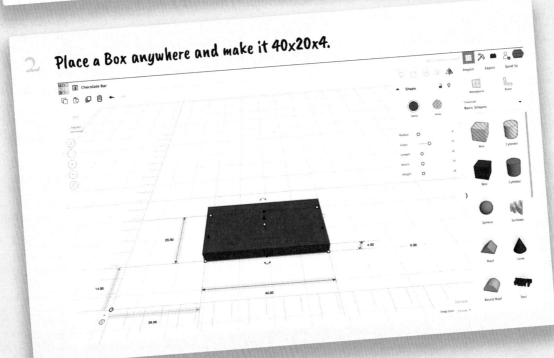

3   Place a Box Hole anywhere and make it 36x16x20.

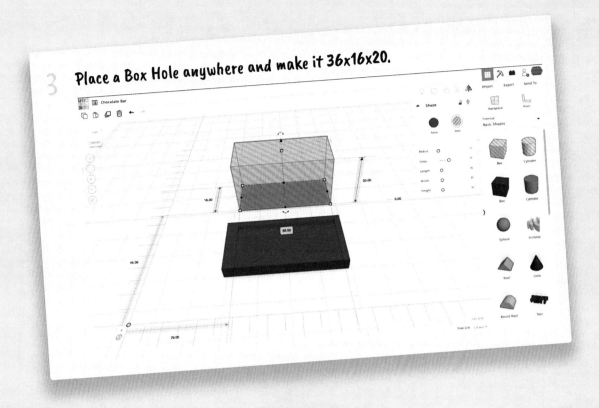

4   Use the Lift tool and raise the Box Hole by 2.

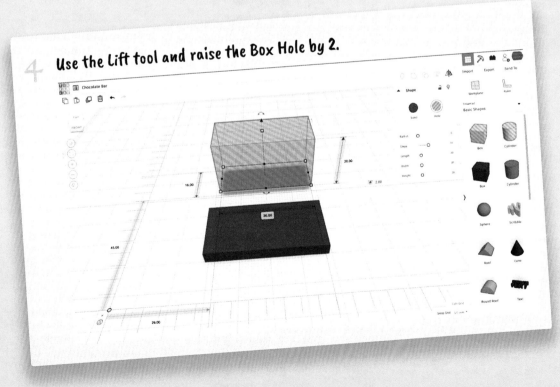

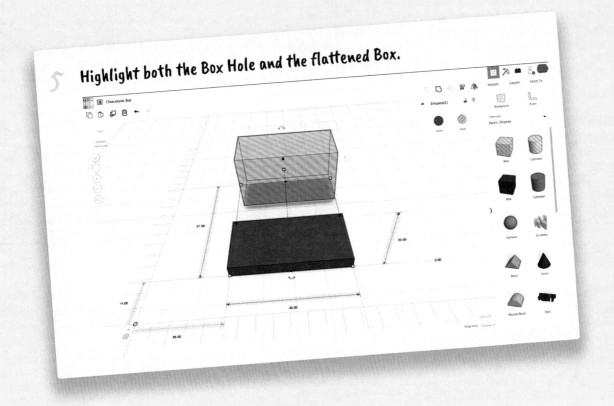

6 Center Align on the left side and bottom center. Click the black dots on the left side and bottom center to align along those two directions.

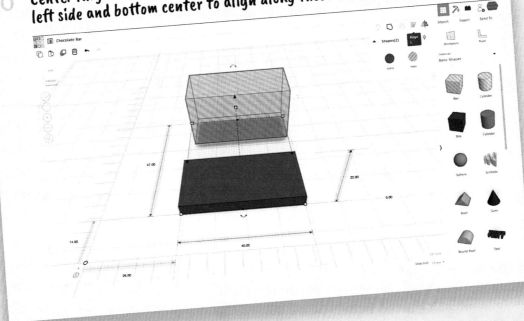

After you click them, the black dots turn gray to signal the objects have been aligned. Click anywhere on the Workplane to exit Align.

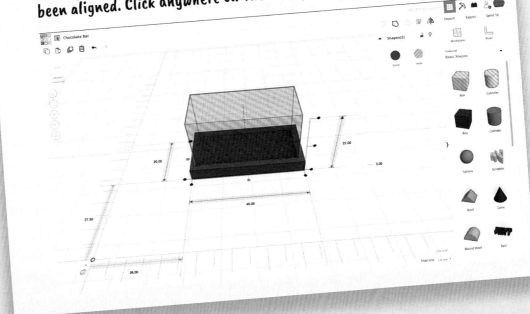

7. **Highlight both objects and Group.**

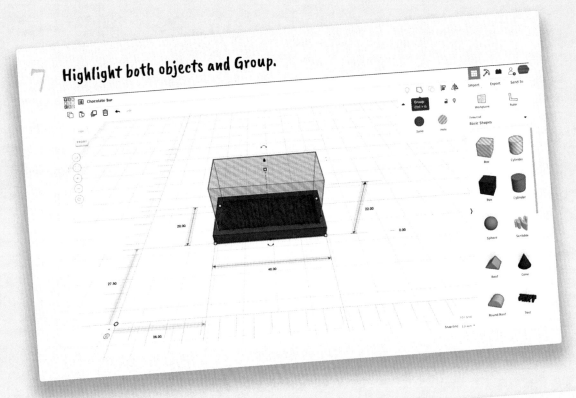

You should now have the base of the chocolate bar with an inset center.

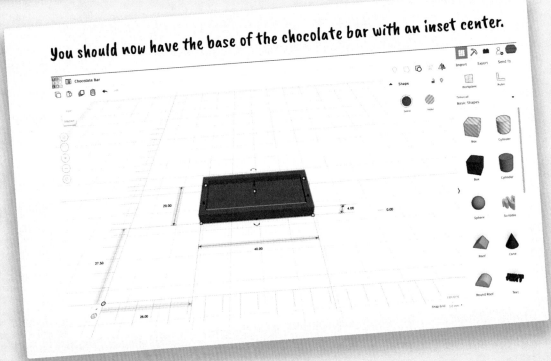

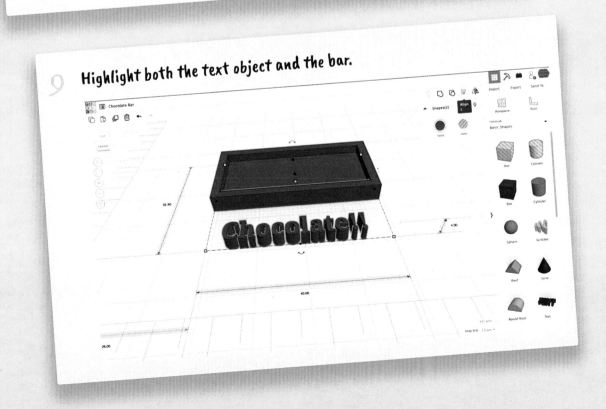

8 Under Basic Shapes, place a Text object on the Workplane. Type "Chocolate!!" and change the size to 30x5x3.

9 Highlight both the text object and the bar.

10 Center Align on the left side and bottom center.

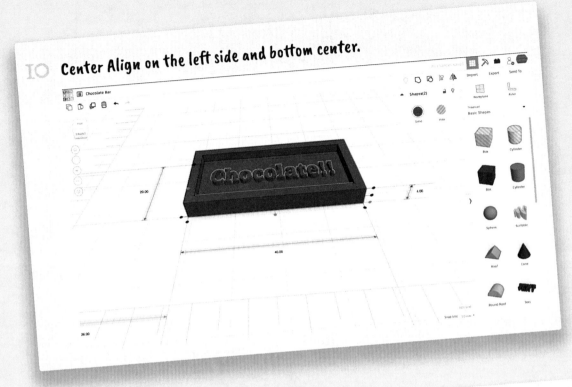

11 Dismiss the Ruler.

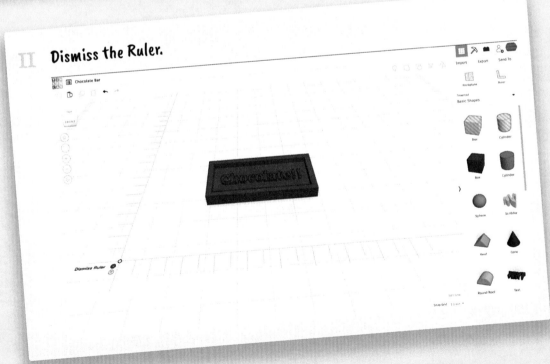

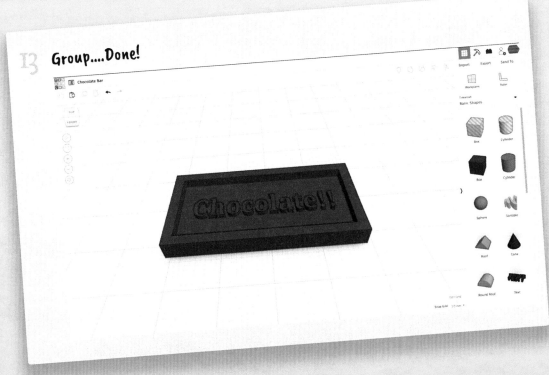

David Seto & Michael Welch

Redbox Hamburger Play Set via Babyshop.com

Wooden Muffin Set With Tray via Growing Kind

CHALLENGE!

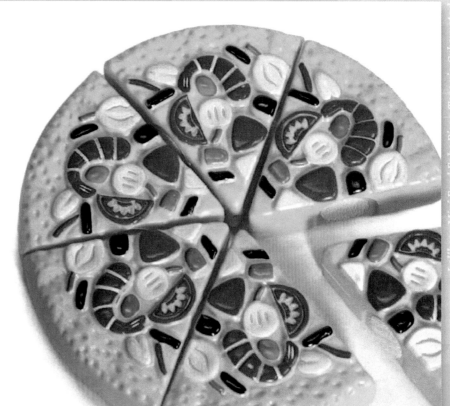

Lolibear Mini Food Fake Pizza Toys via Cyberustad

Oide Burger

Astro by Florida Atlantic University

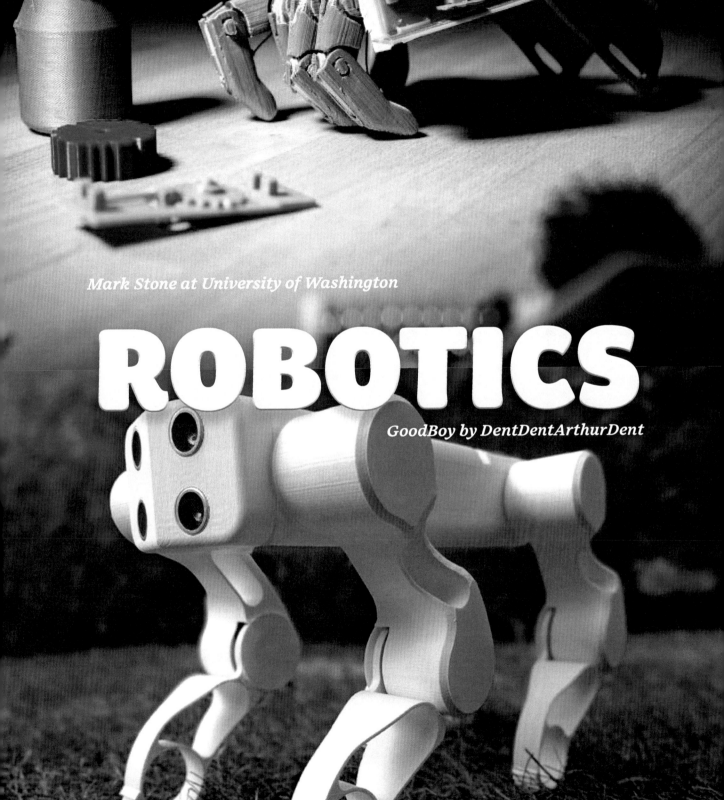

Mark Stone at University of Washington

ROBOTICS

GoodBoy by DentDentArthurDent

The Black Center Point is important here because both sides of the base should be symmetrical. I usually encourage the students to see if they can design the rest of the finger or even the entire robot's hand.

Robot Finger Tip

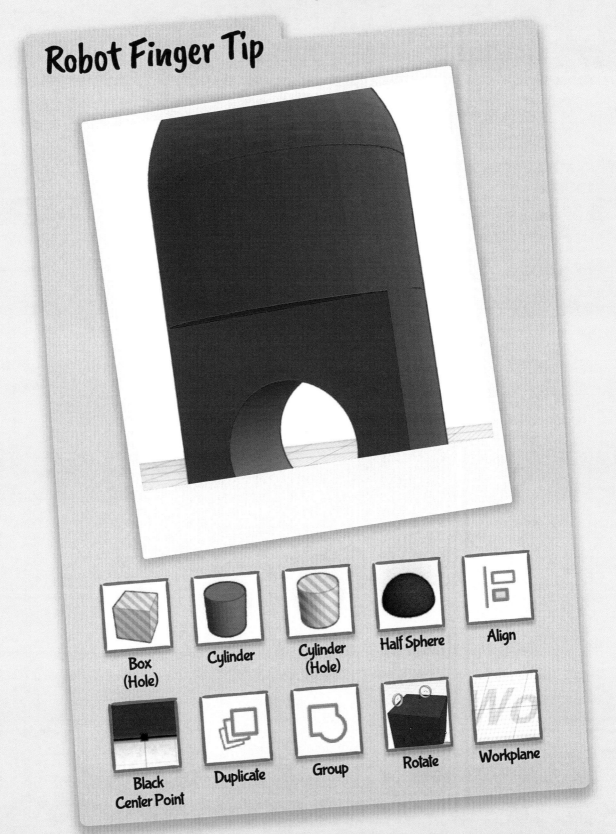

Box (Hole)

Cylinder

Cylinder (Hole)

Half Sphere

Align

Black Center Point

Duplicate

Group

Rotate

Workplane

1 Place a solid Cylinder at the center of four large squares in the Workplane, making sure the Cylinder's Black Center Point lines up with a heavy line on the Workplane.

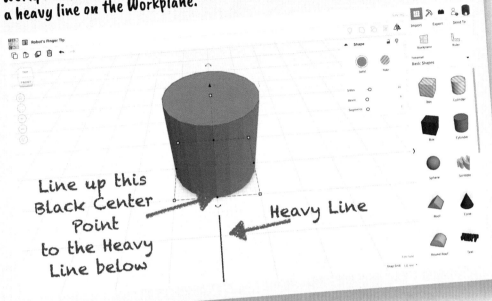

Line up this Black Center Point to the Heavy Line below

Heavy Line

2 Increase Sides to 64 to smooth out the Cylinder.

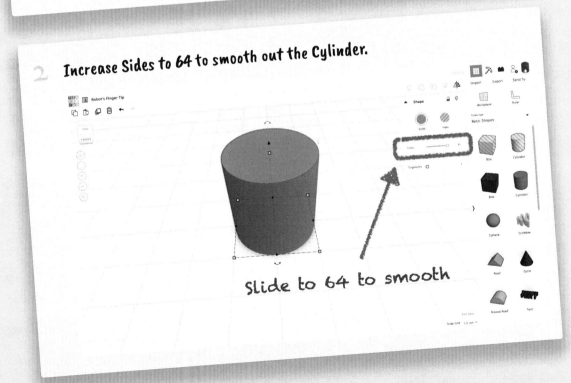

Slide to 64 to smooth

3 Place a Box Hole so its bottom left corner falls on the Cylinder's Black Center Point.

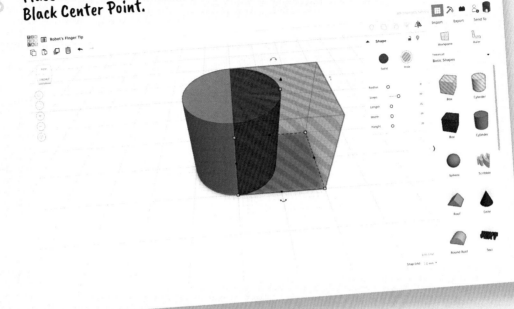

4 Use the Right Arrow Key on your keyboard to move the Box Hole 5 small squares to the right of the Cylinder's Black Center Point.

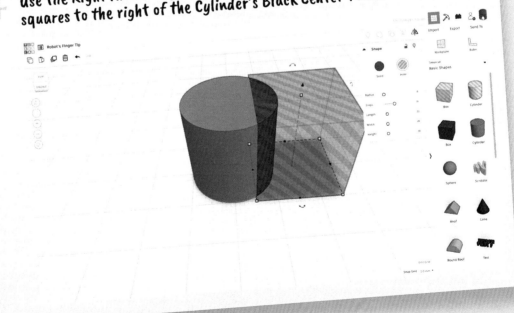

5 Duplicate the Box Hole and use your keyboard's arrow keys to move the new Box Hole 5 small squares to the left of the Cylinder's Black Center Point.

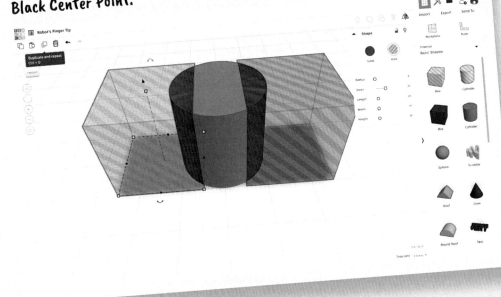

6 Highlight all, then Group.

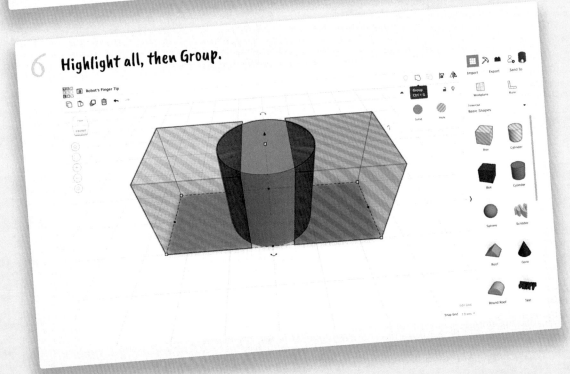

When you Group a Solid with a Hole, the Hole cuts away part of the Solid.

7 **Place a Cylinder Hole on the Workplane. Slide the Sides to 64, and make it 10x10 on the bottom.**

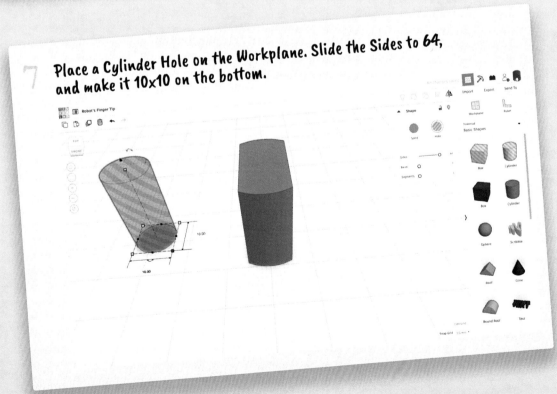

8

Rotate the Cylinder Hole 90 degrees to a horizontal position with one end pointing to the original Cylinder.

9

Highlight all then Center Align on the X, Y and Z axes. Click anywhere in the Workplane to exit Align.

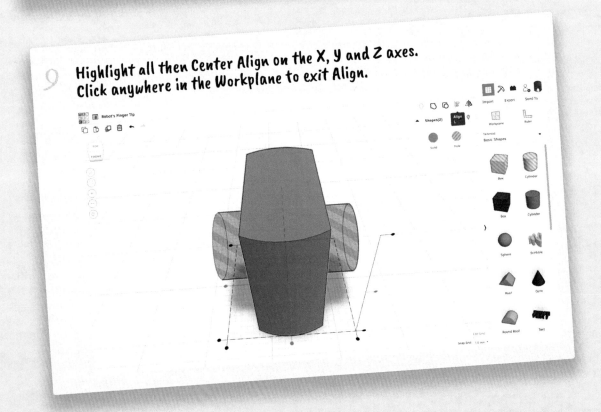

IO **Highlight both objects and Group.**

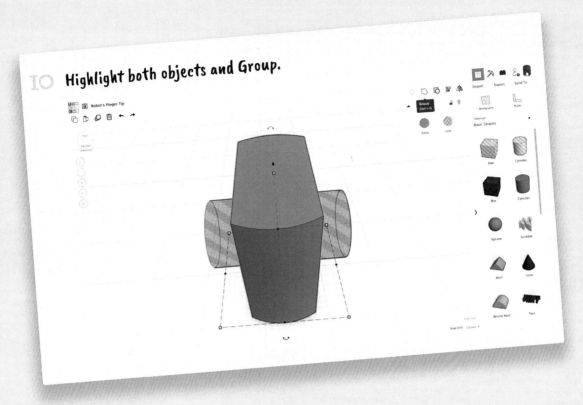

Once again, the Group Tool has knocked a hole in the finger joint.

11

Place a new solid Cylinder on the Workplane. Set the Sides to 64 and apply a height of 10, then Lift it up 20.

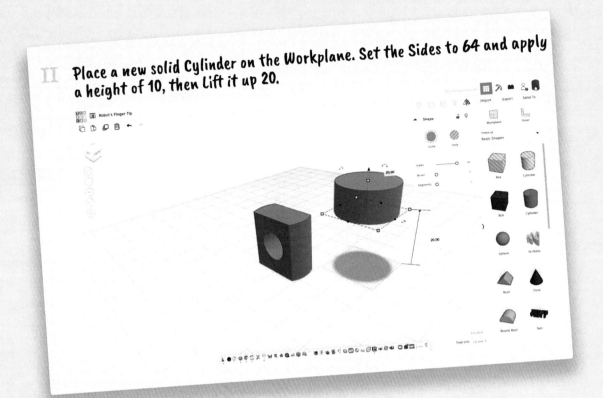

12

Place a Half Sphere on the Workplane and Lift 30.

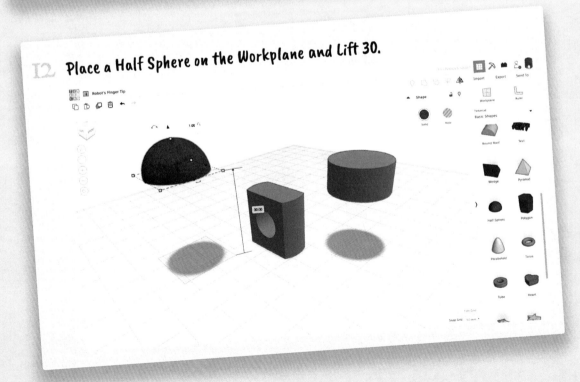

Highlight all and center Align on the bottom and side on the Workplane...

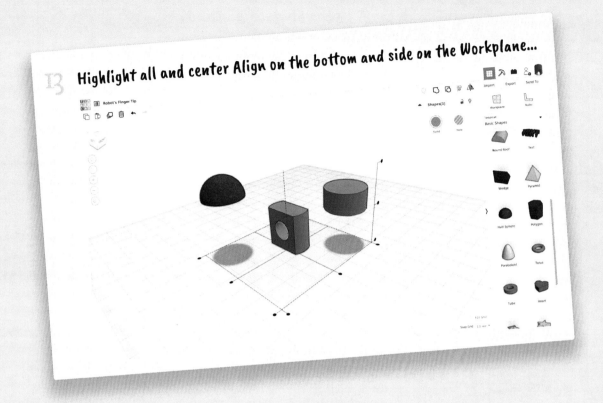

...and click outside to exit Align. This brings all the pieces together!

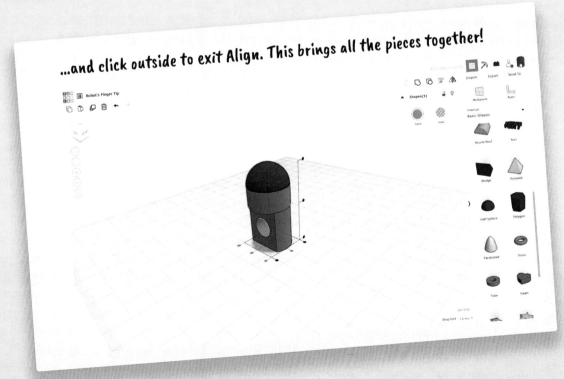

14 Highlight all.

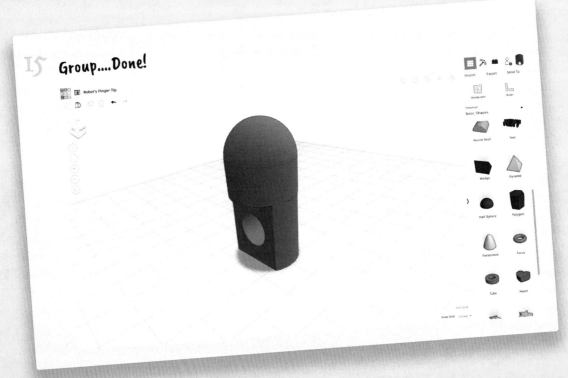

15 Group....Done!

Avengers 1:1 Iron Man Right Hand Gauntlet Glove 3D Lightable LED Light Cosplay High Quality by AliExpress

InMoov Finger Prosthetic! by GAEL LANGEVIN

CHALLENGE!

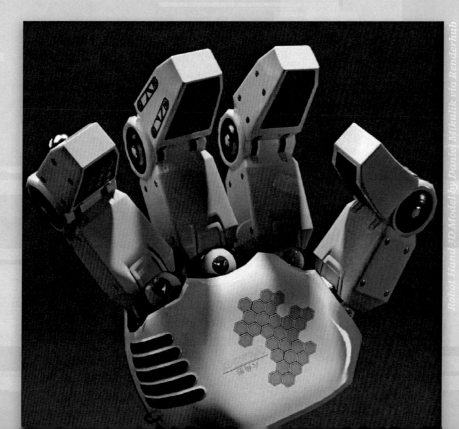

Robot Hand 3D Model by Daniel Mikulik via Renderhub

Northern Pike RC Airplane by localfiend

Curtiss P40 Warhawk by 3Dmodeling

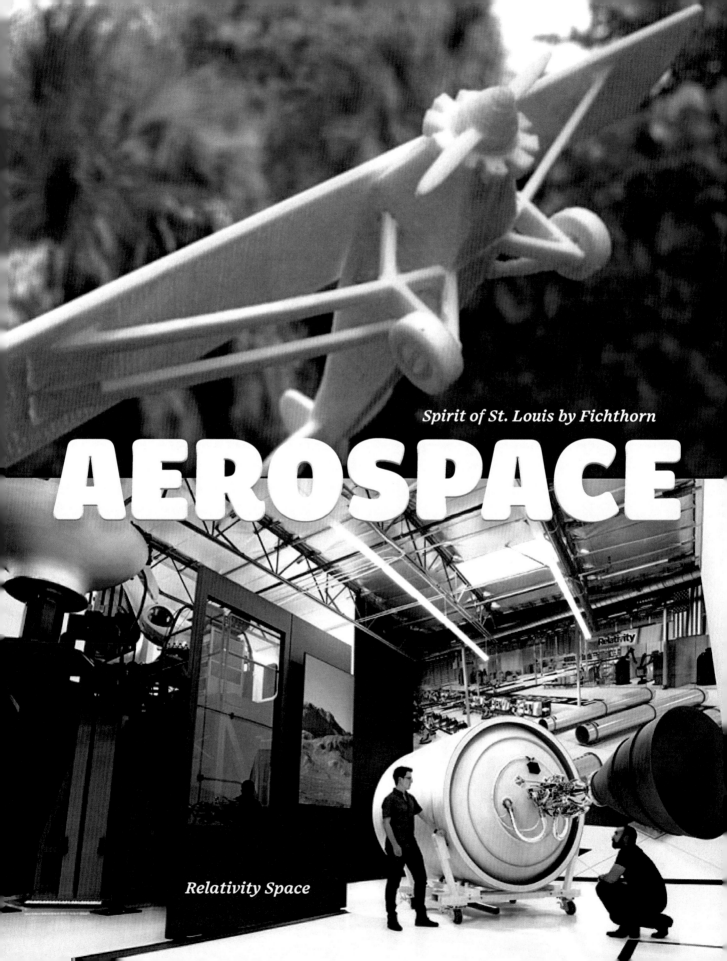

AEROSPACE

Spirit of St. Louis by Fichthorn

Relativity Space

We introduce the Mirror tool to create the fins quickly.

Can you see that the vertical part of each fin extends into the rocket's body?

This ensures the fins and the fuselage are properly joined during 3D printing.

Rocket

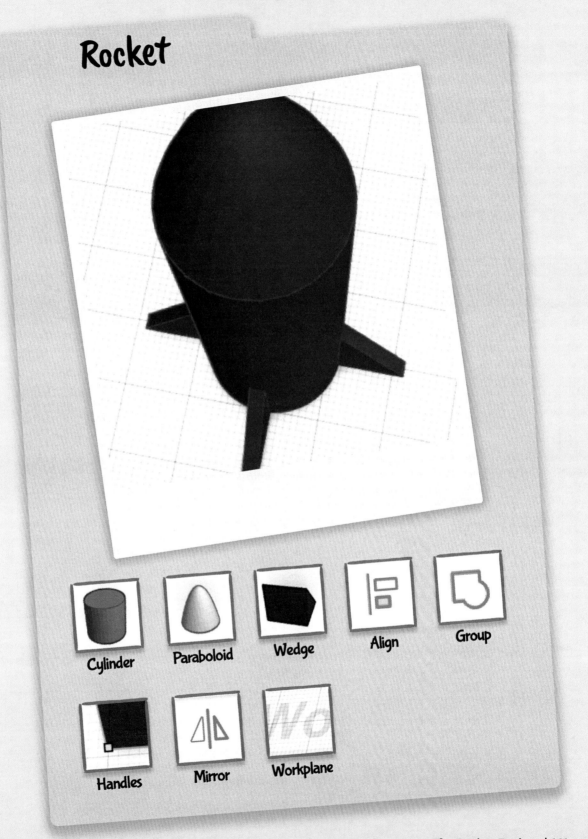

Cylinder　　**Paraboloid**　　**Wedge**　　**Align**　　**Group**

Handles　　**Mirror**　　**Workplane**

1. We are going to make the four fins first, so, under Basic Shapes, put a Wedge on the Workplane.

2. Give it a depth of 11 and width of 2 (the height of the fin faces Front).

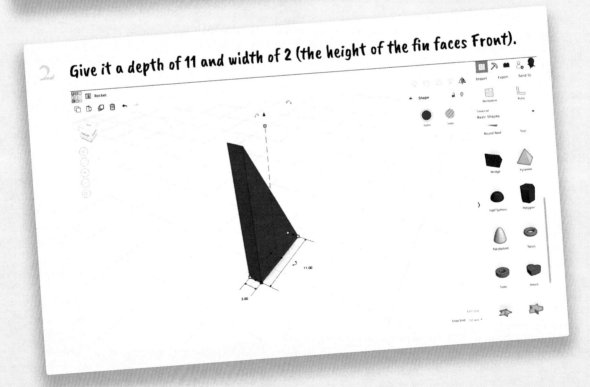

3   Line up the Black Center Point of the fin's width to a heavy line on the Workplane.

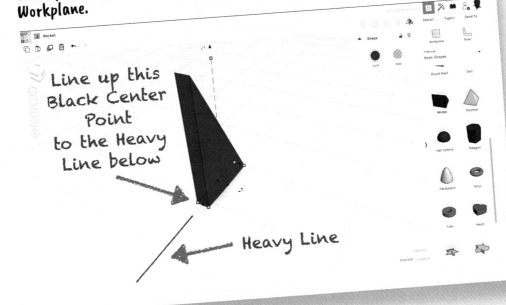

Line up this Black Center Point to the Heavy Line below

Heavy Line

4   Note that the length of the fin's base is 11 because we want all four fins to be embedded into the rocket's main body later on. So place the fin to cover 10 small squares with the remainder spilling over into a large square.

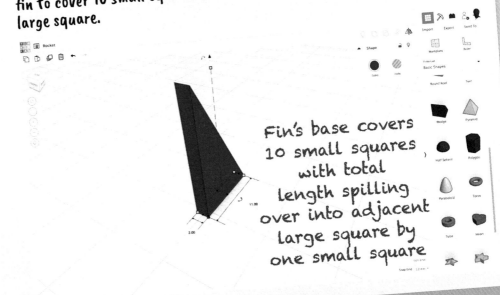

Fin's base covers 10 small squares with total length spilling over into adjacent large square by one small square

5 Duplicate the fin and use the Down Arrow Key on your keyboard to slide the copy across two large squares to the Front.

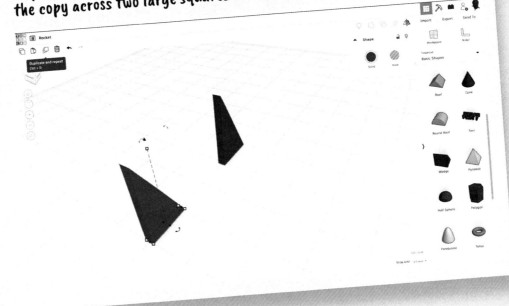

6 Use the Mirror tool to flip the front fin...

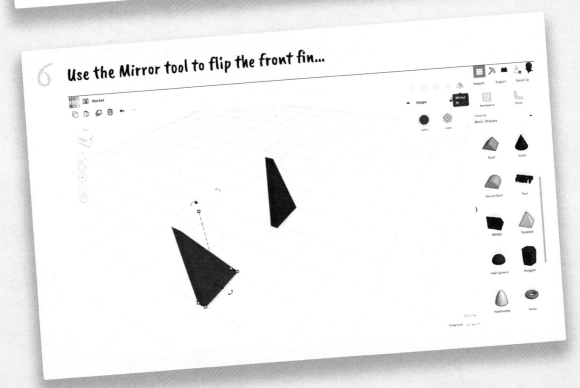

...and note the vertical ends of each fin now face each other, with 18 small squares between them.

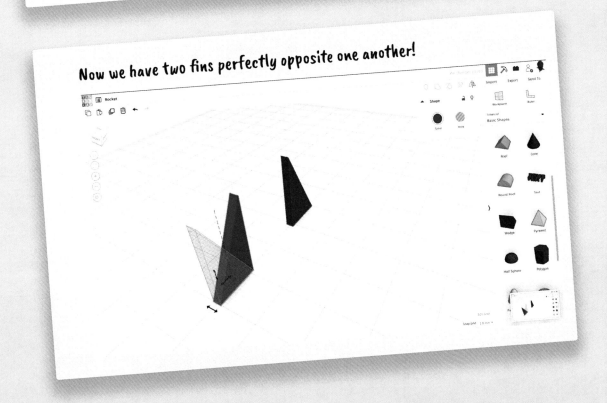

Now we have two fins perfectly opposite one another!

7 Highlight both fins, then Duplicate and Rotate the new fins 90 degrees. Click outside to exit the Rotate tool.

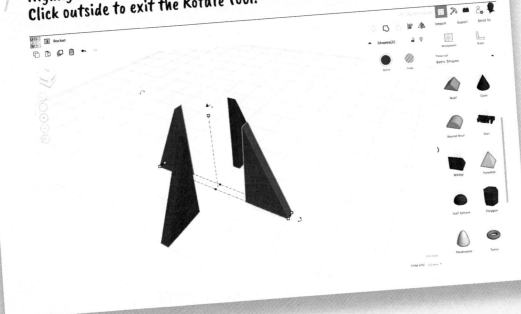

8 Highlight all four fins and Group.

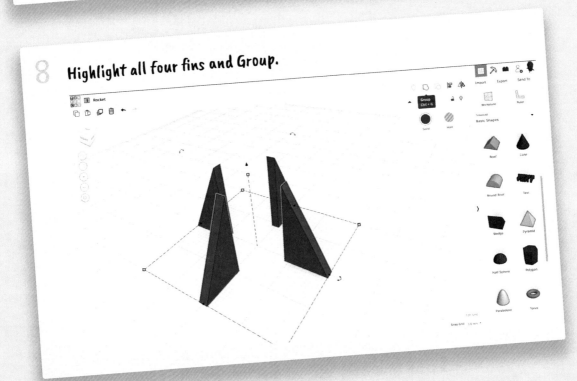

9   Put a Cylinder on the Workplane:
     set Sides to 64 to smooth and change the height to 70.

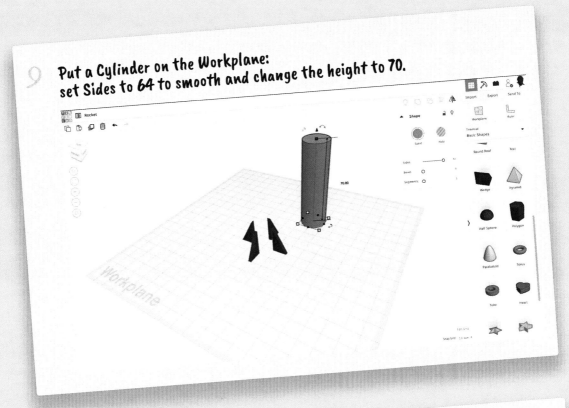

IO   Put a Paraboloid on the Workplane and use the Lift tool to raise by 70.

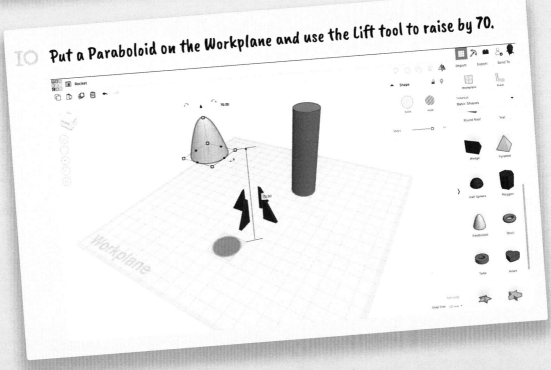

II **Highlight all and use the Align tool to center on the bottom two sides.**

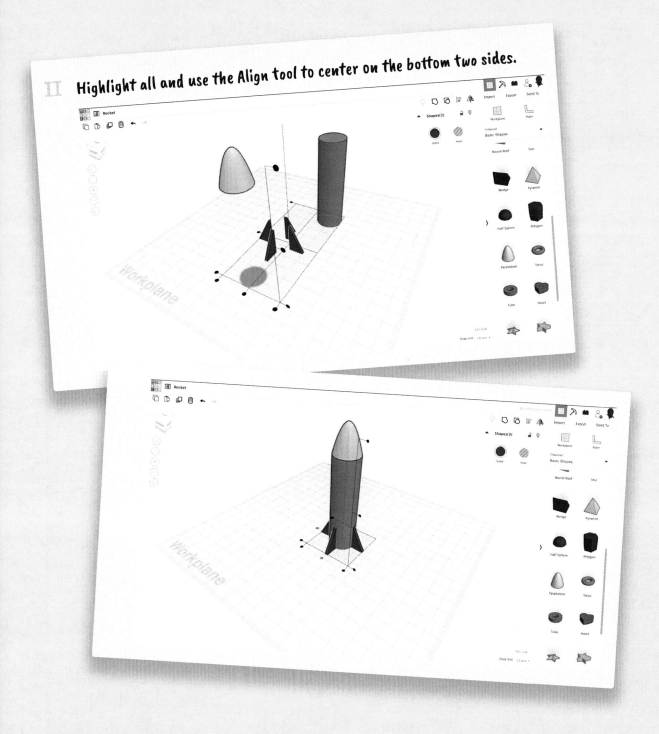

12 Highlight all.

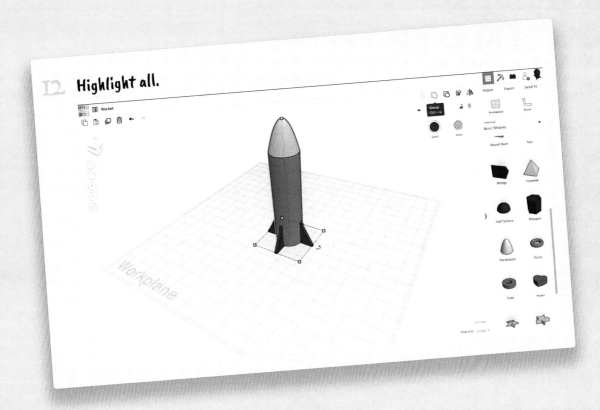

13 Group....Done!

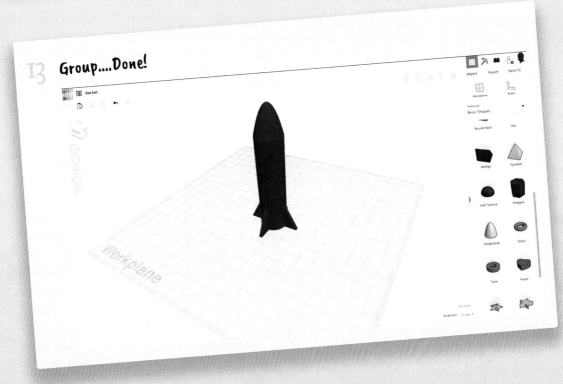

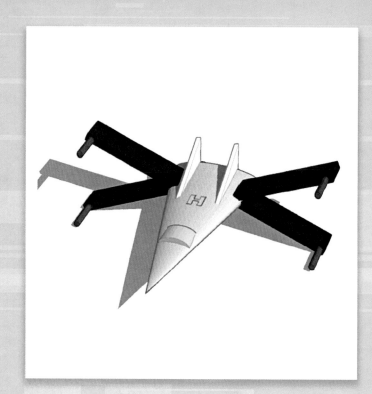

CHALLENGE!

Divergent 3D Blade

Mini 1936 Grand Prix by Audi

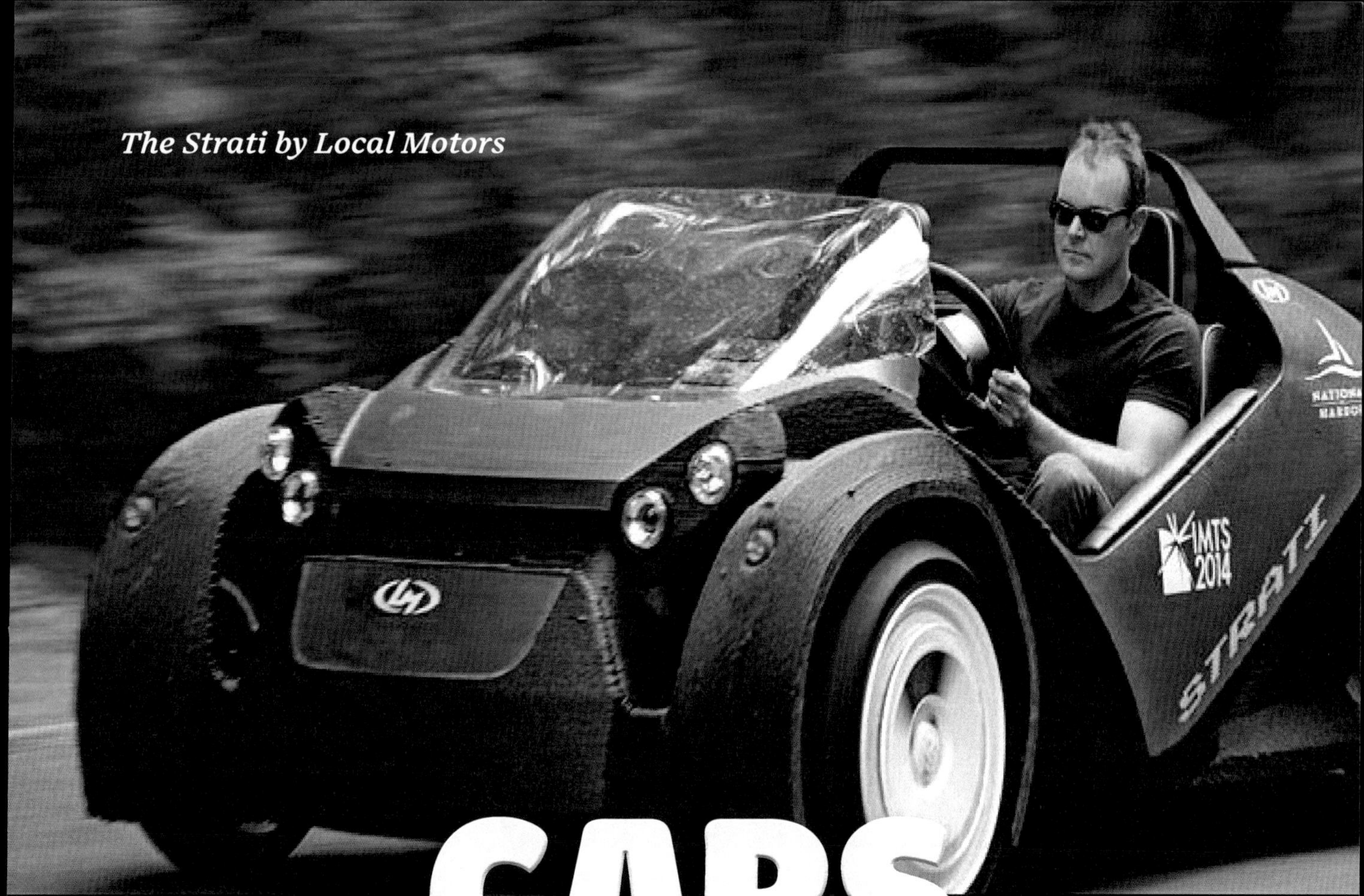

The Strati by Local Motors

CARS

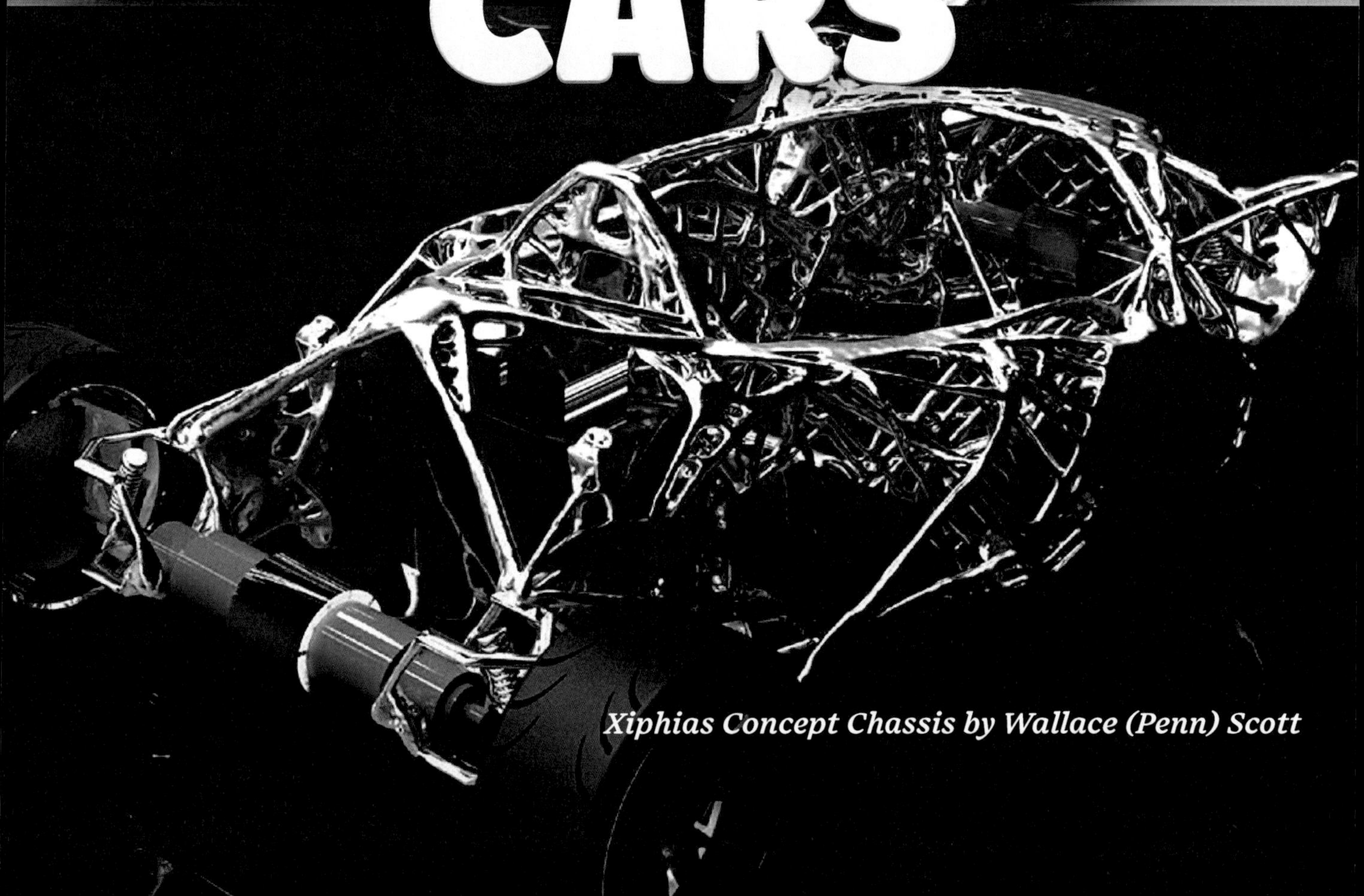

Xiphias Concept Chassis by Wallace (Penn) Scott

This model will demonstrate how flexible the Workplane can be.

It doesn't just sit passively on the "floor." You can place this "floor" anywhere.

Car

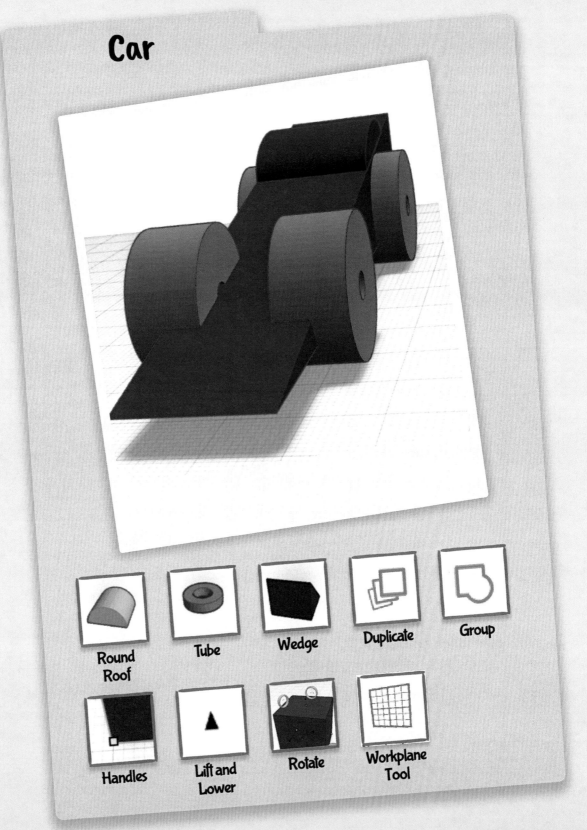

Round Roof   **Tube**   **Wedge**   **Duplicate**   **Group**

Handles   **Lift and Lower**   **Rotate**   **Workplane Tool**

1. Under Basic Shapes, put a Wedge on the Workplane.

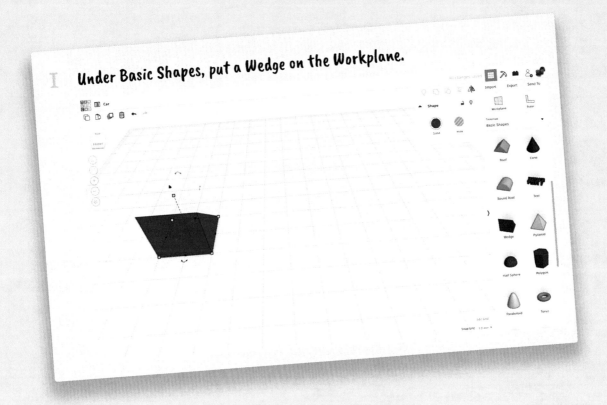

2. Rotate the Wedge 90 degrees so that its back faces right.

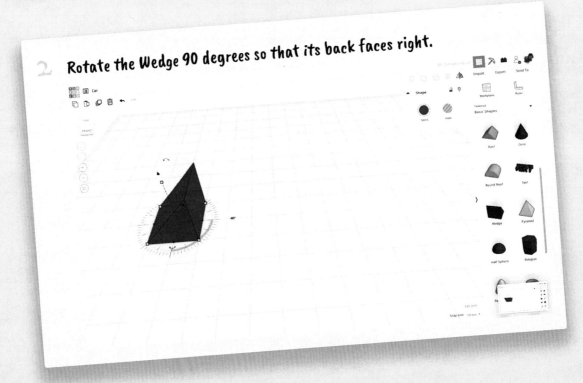

3 Give the Wedge a length of 100.

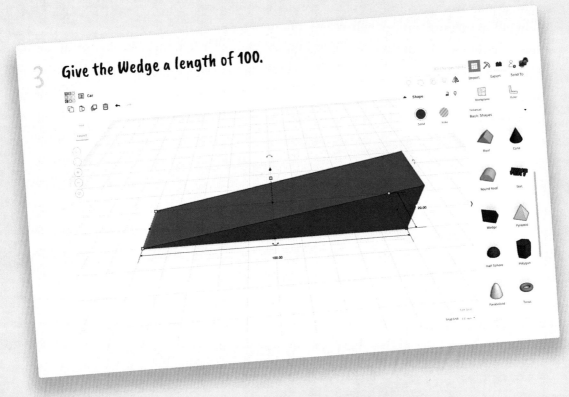

4 Put a Round Roof on the Workplane and change the height to 5.

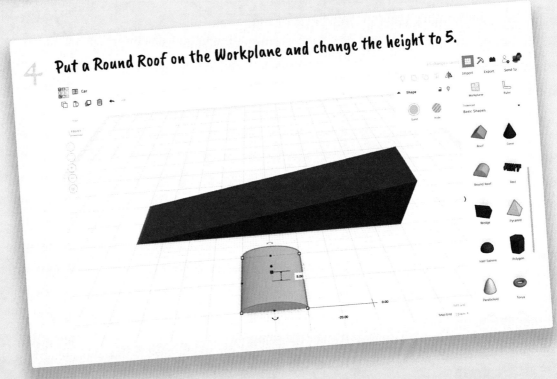

5 Position the Round Roof towards the back of the car's body.

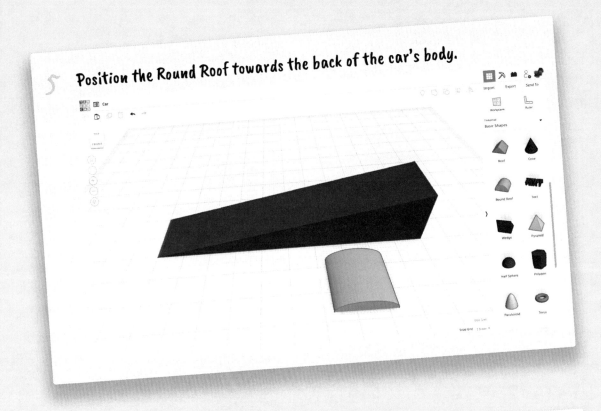

6 Use the Lift tool to raise the Round Roof higher than the car's body.

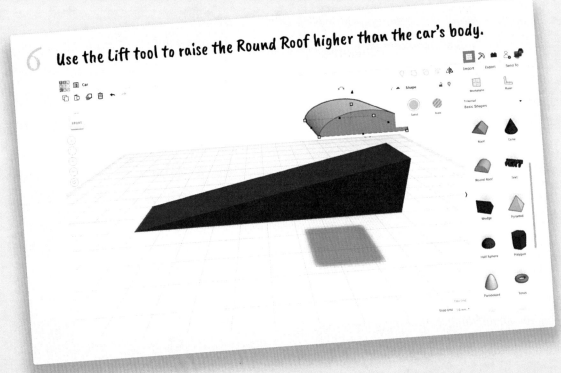

7 **Highlight the roof and car body, then center Align along the car's length.**

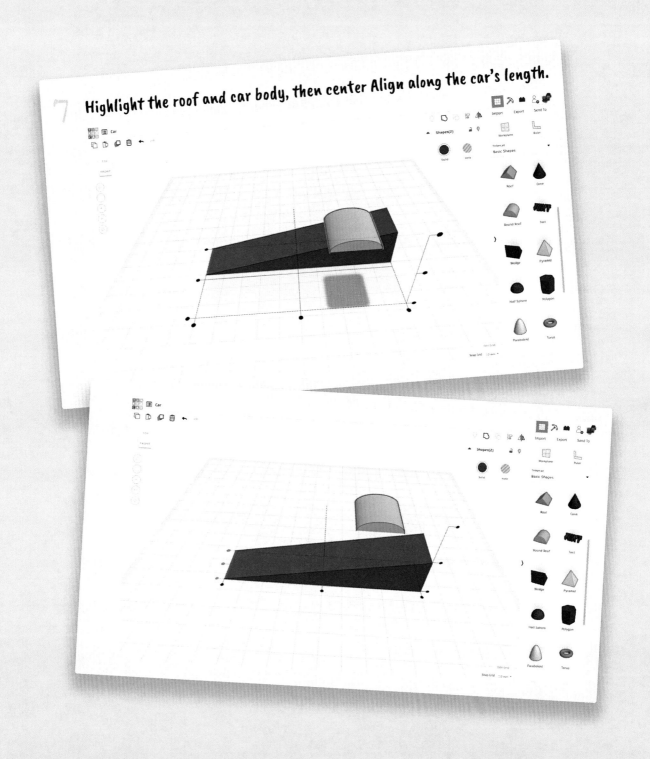

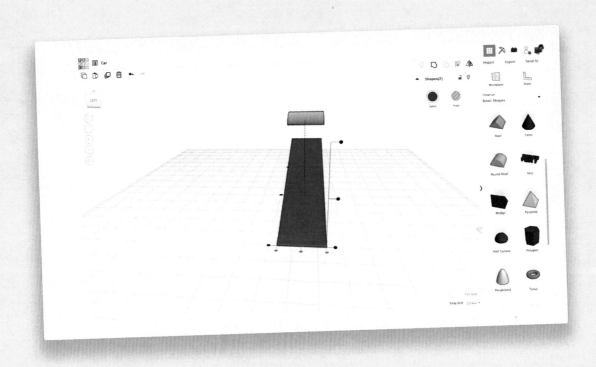

8 Rotate the Round Roof 11 degrees counterclockwise.
We want the Round Roof to rest on the angled wedge without any gaps.

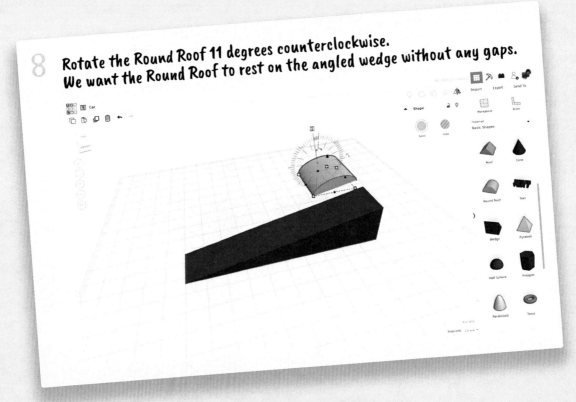

9 **Place a Workplane tool on top of the car's body.**

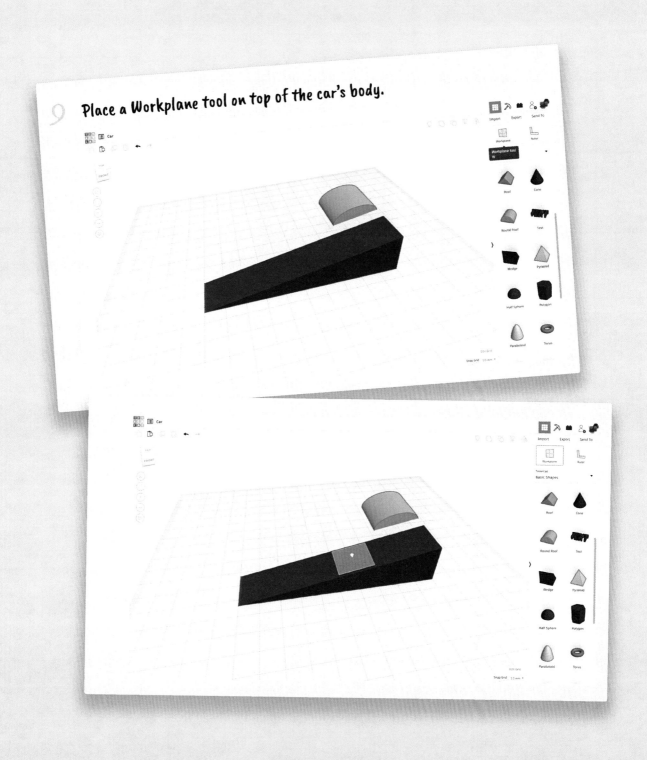

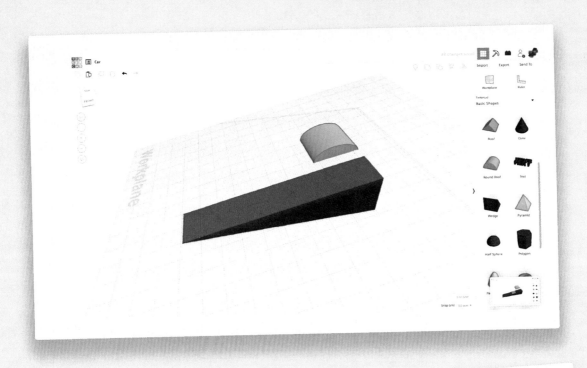

10 Click the Round Roof and press D to drop it onto the angled Workplane.

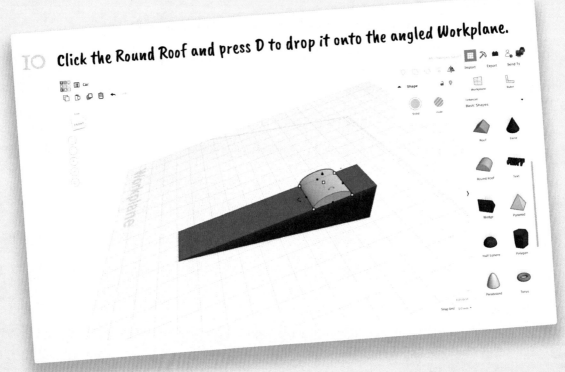

11 Grab another Workplane tool and place it back to the original level to restore it.

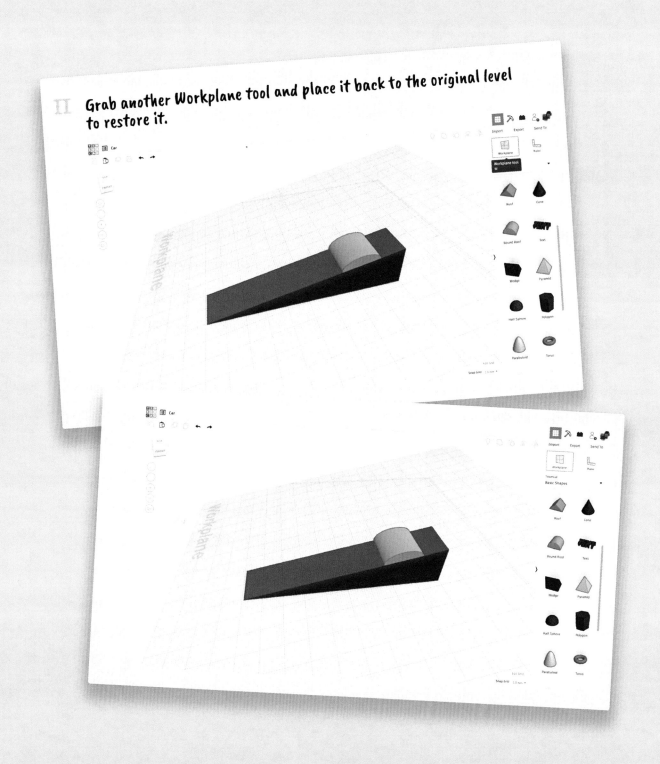

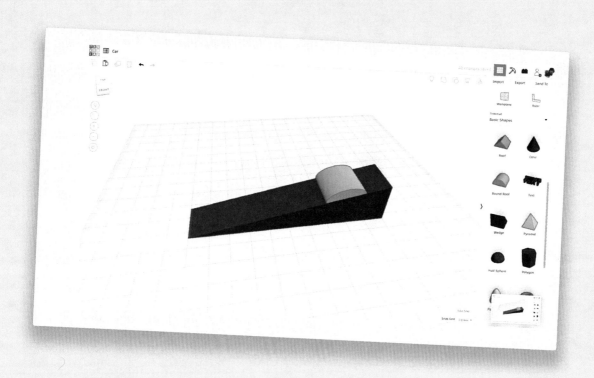

12 Highlight both objects and Group.

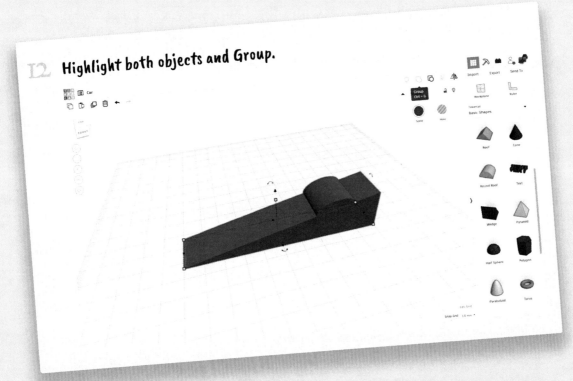

13 Orbit to the front of the car and line up the front left corner of the car to a corner of a large square in the Workplane.

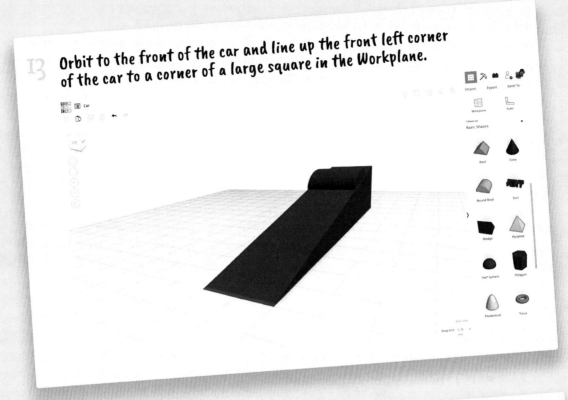

14 Under Basic Shapes, place a Tube two large squares from the front of the car.

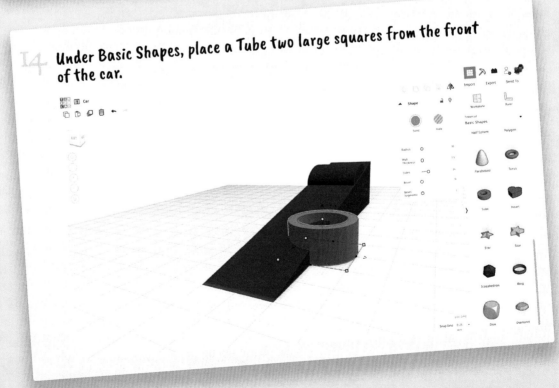

15 Increase Sides to 64 and apply a Wall Thickness of 8. Make sure the Tube's Black Center Point lines up with a heavy line on the Workplane.

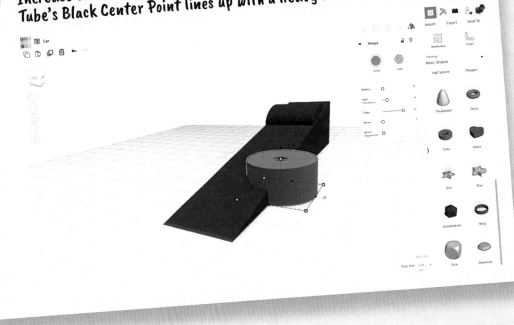

16 Rotate the tire 90 degrees upright.

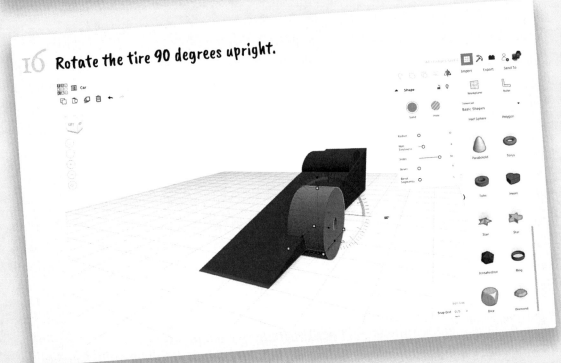

17 Duplicate the tire and move it to the car's right side.
Make sure its Black Center Point lines up with the car's body.

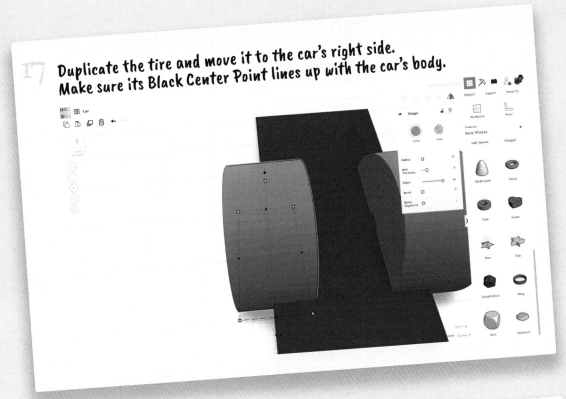

18 Holding down Shift key and Group both tires.

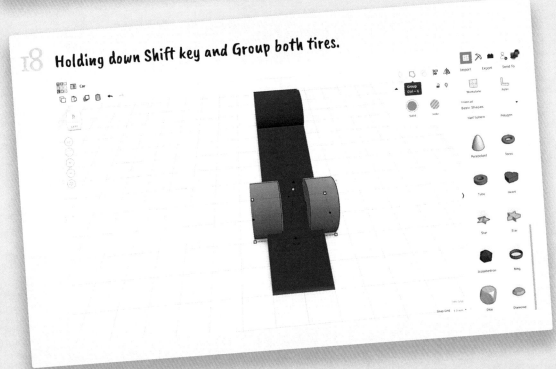

19 Highlight and Duplicate both tires, then slide them back to behind the Round Roof to create the car's rear wheels.

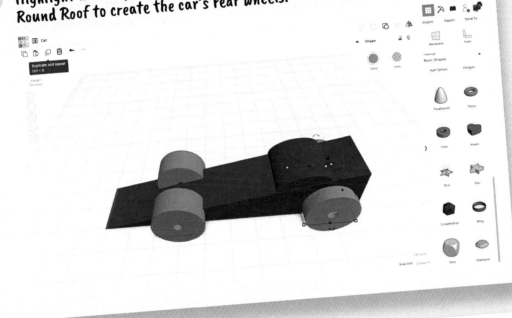

20 Highlight all, then use the Lift tool to raise the car above the Workplane. Press D to drop and we're done!

F1 TOY ART RACECAR CAR RACE DESIGN / AGCREATION3D on Cults3D.com

CHALLENGE!

Push Racing Car Wooden Toy / Botanica Works

BAIO Wooden Formula One Racing Car

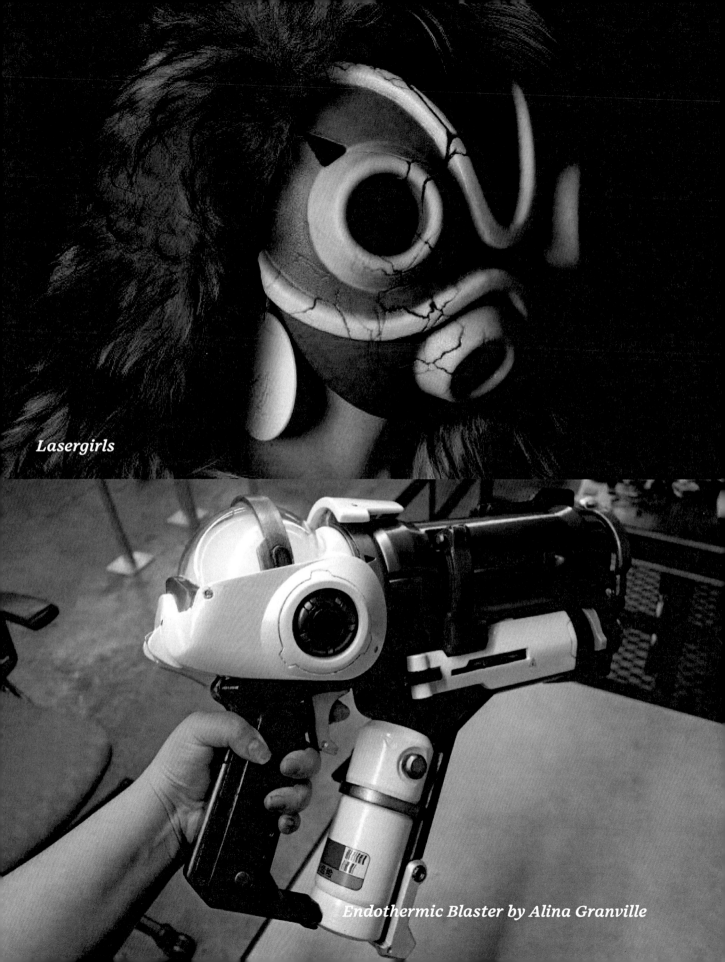

Lasergirls

Endothermic Blaster by Alina Granville

K-2SO Cosplay by Jeremy Simon and Ivan Owen

COSPLAY

Mike Hall

Located on the bottom right of the working screen, the Snap Grid tool is for the real, nit picky designer who demands exact placement of certain objects.

It's not commonly used, but for the Wand, which requires exact placement of its handle, the Snap Grid tool is very important.

Wand

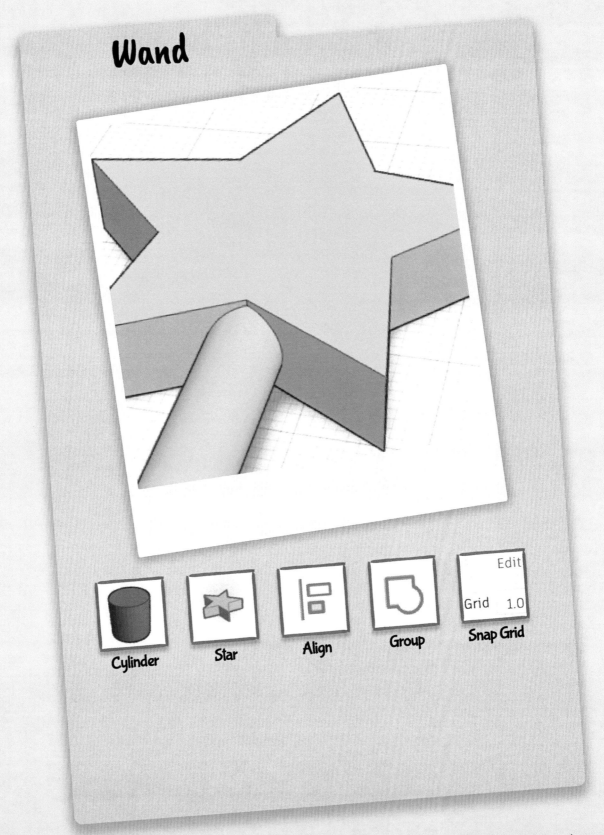

Cylinder   Star   Align   Group   Snap Grid

1. Under Basic Shapes, put a Star on the Workplane.

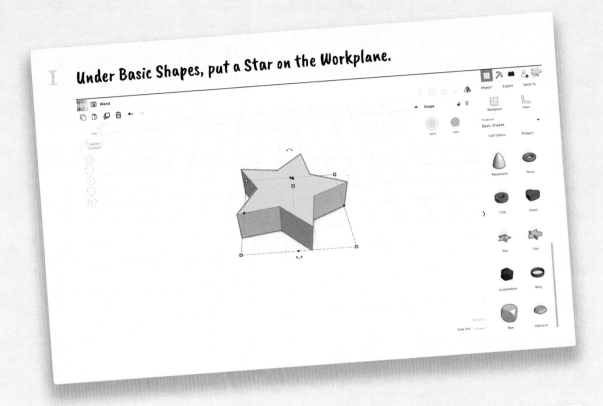

2. Rotate the Star 18 degrees counterclockwise so the bottom tips of the star line up with a horizontal line.

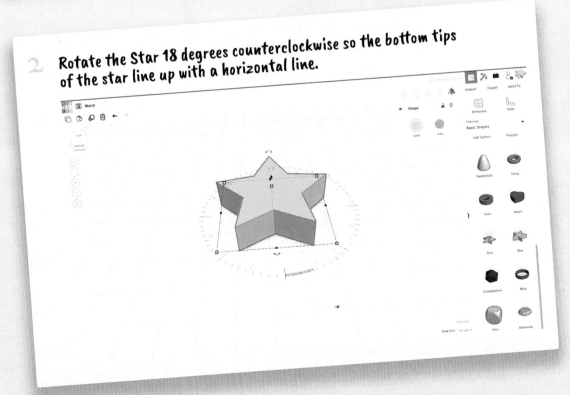

Set the height of the Star to 7.

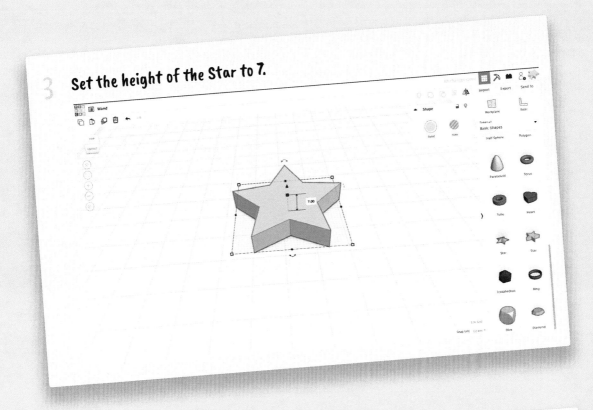

Next, under Basic Shapes, put a Cylinder on the Workplane.

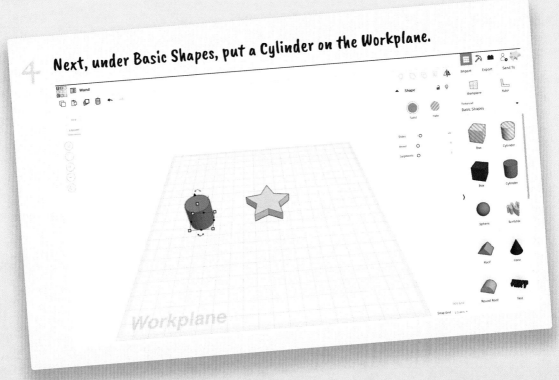

5   **For the Cylinder, increase the Sides to 64, set the bottom to 6x6, and give it a height of 70.**

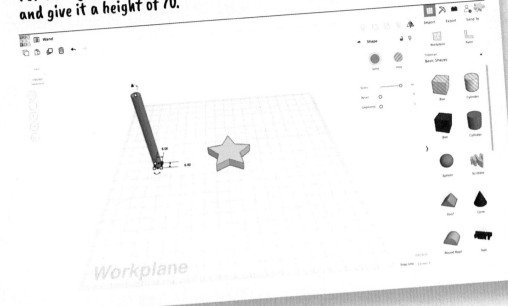

6   **Orbit to a side view, then rotate the Cylinder 90 degrees. Press D to drop.**

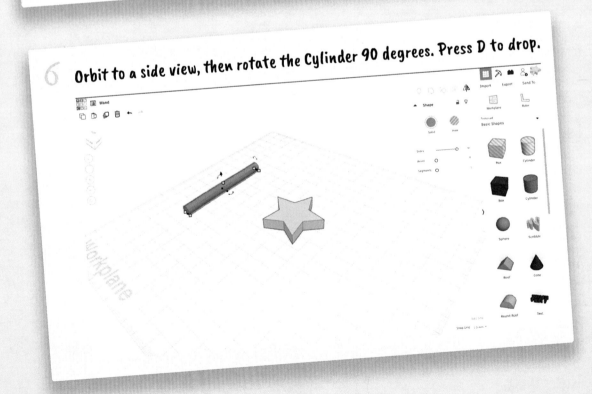

7 **Slide one end of the Cylinder into the Star.**

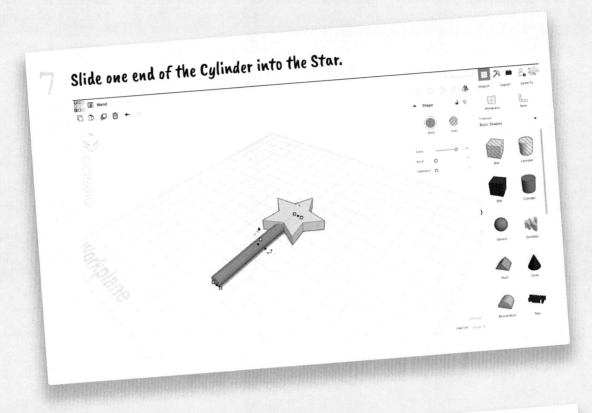

8 **Highlight both objects and center Align along the length.**

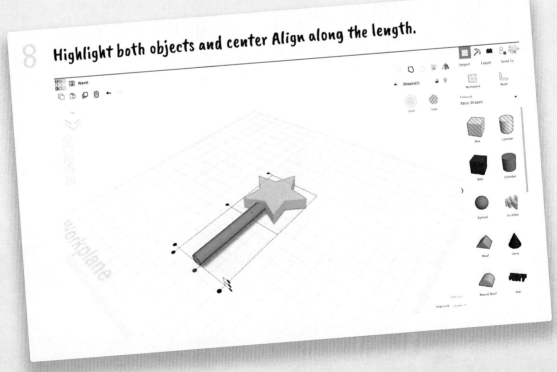

The Star is now aligned properly to the wand.

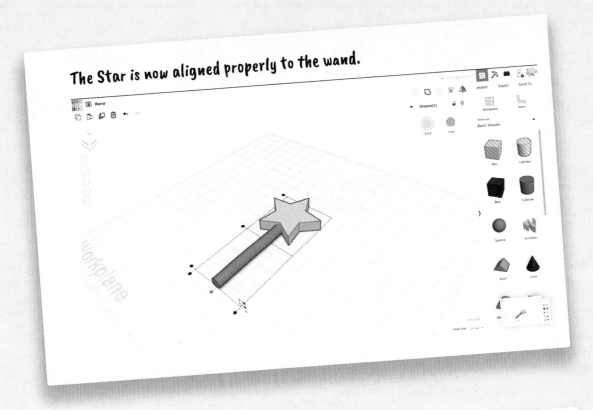

Change the Snap Grid on the bottom right to 0.5mm.

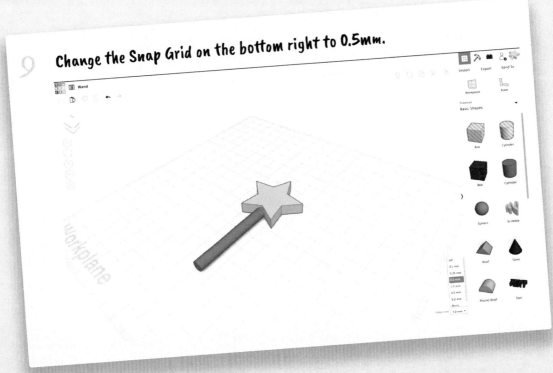

IO **Use the Lift tool to raise the Cylinder by 0.5.**

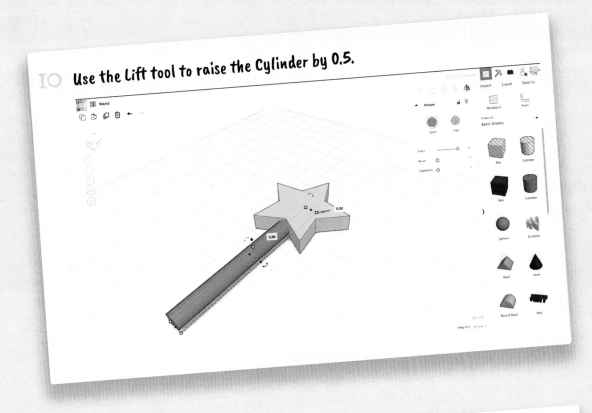

II **Highlight both objects again.**

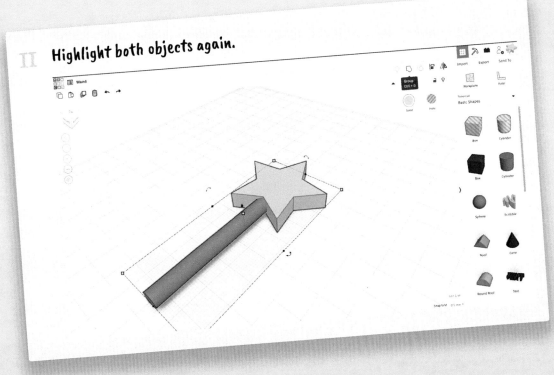

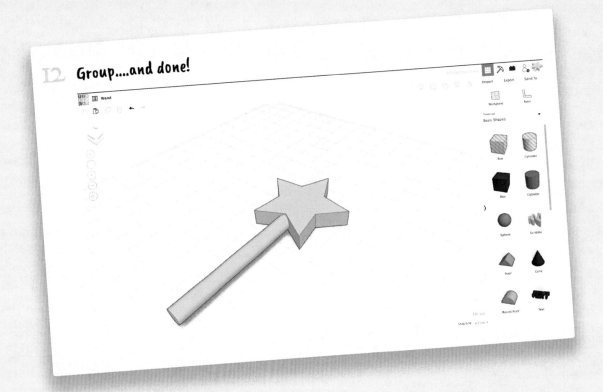

CHALLENGE!

Appendix A:
Syllabus & Slides

I hope you can use these presentation slides to start off your class.

http://3dprintingcookbook.com/slides/tinkercad

Appendix B:
Handouts for In-Class Use

Printing out these pages and distributing to each of your students will also help them follow along during your lesson. Even if they missed a single mouse click, they can resort to these "recipes" to get them back on track. Also, you will find these condensed instructions are a great way to manage situations when multiple questions come up at the same time. When the students get stuck, as they surely will, the answers are already right in front of them. The handouts in the following pages can be used directly or you can download digital copies from the book's website: http://3dprintingcookbook.com/handouts/tinkercad

Navigation

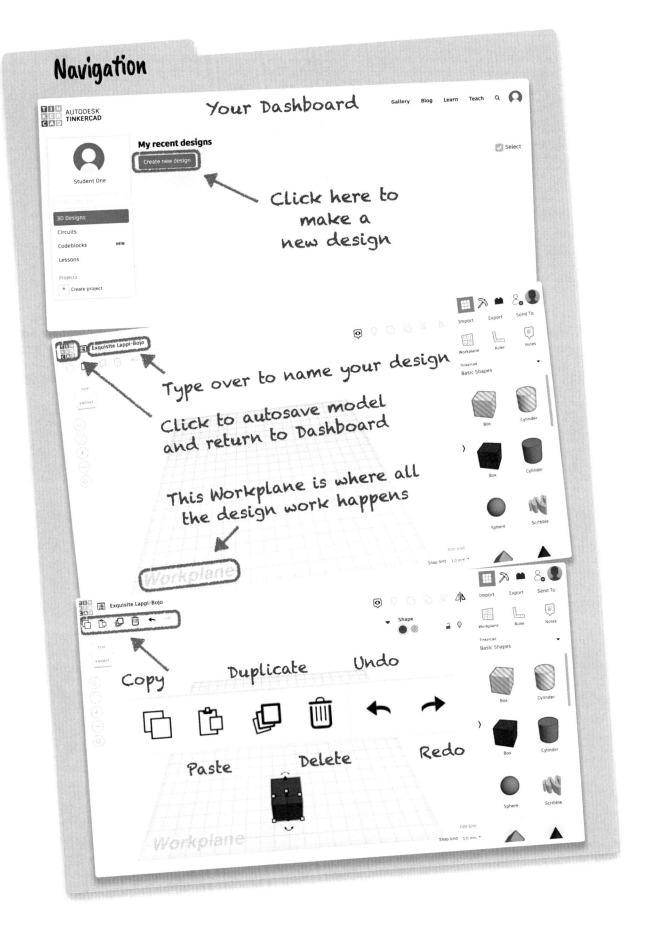

Your Dashboard

Gallery   Blog   Learn   Teach

Student One

My recent designs

Create new design

3D Designs
Circuits
Codeblocks   NEW
Lessons

Projects
+ Create project

Click here to
make a
new design

Exquisite Lappi-Bojo

Import   Export   Send To

Workplane   Ruler   Notes

Tinkercad
Basic Shapes

Box   Cylinder

Box   Cylinder

Sphere   Scribble

Type over to name your design

Click to autosave model
and return to Dashboard

This Workplane is where all
the design work happens

Workplane

Copy   Duplicate   Undo

Paste   Delete   Redo

Workplane

Navigation

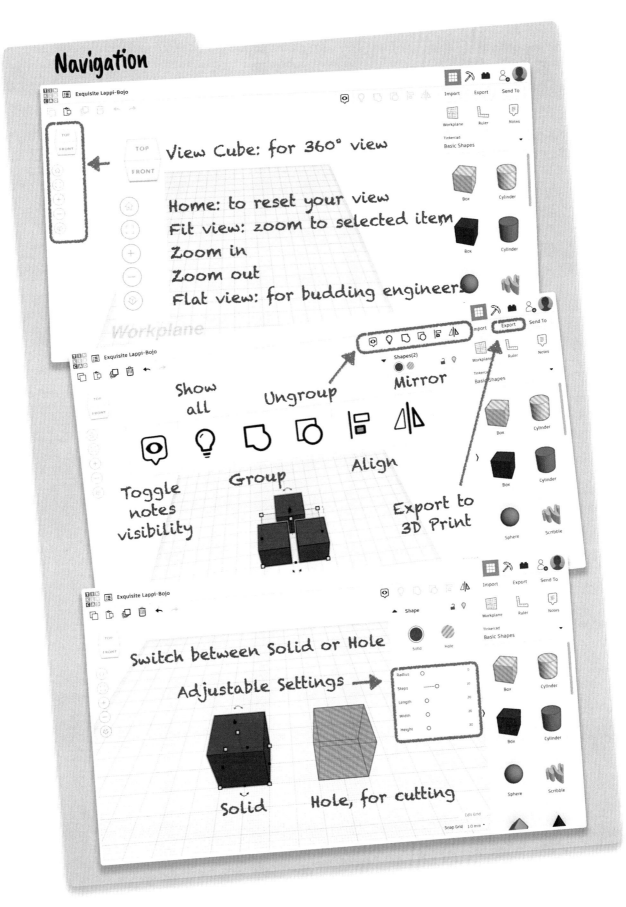

View Cube: for 360° view

Home: to reset your view
Fit view: zoom to selected item
Zoom in
Zoom out
Flat view: for budding engineers

Show all

Ungroup

Mirror

Toggle notes visibility

Group

Align

Export to 3D Print

Switch between Solid or Hole

Adjustable Settings →

Solid

Hole, for cutting

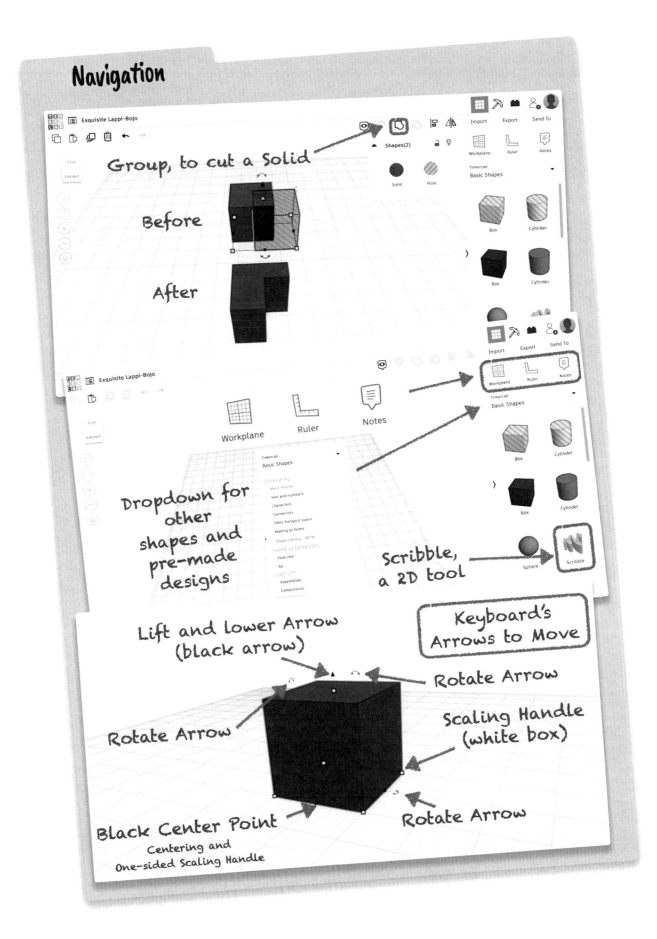

Group, to cut a Solid

Before

After

Workplane

Ruler

Notes

Dropdown for other shapes and pre-made designs

Scribble, a 2D tool

Lift and lower Arrow (black arrow)

Keyboard's Arrows to Move

Rotate Arrow

Rotate Arrow

Scaling Handle (white box)

Black Center Point
Centering and One-sided Scaling Handle

Rotate Arrow

Step-by-Step

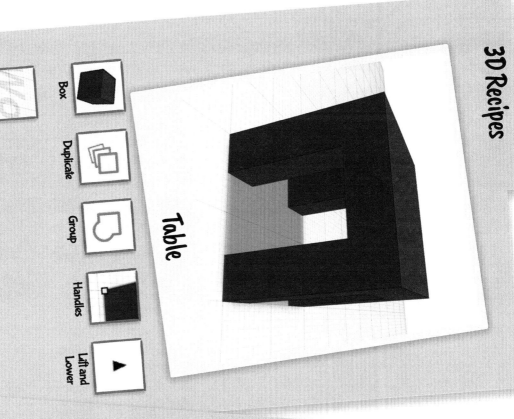

Table

Workplane

Box

Duplicate

Group

Handles

Lift and Lower

1. Pick four large squares on Workplane.
2. Place Box inside four squares.
3. Use Handle to make 5x5 bottom to one corner of four large squares.
4. Duplicate.
5. Move duplicate to other side of four large squares.
6. Highlight both.
7. Duplicate.
8. Move both duplicates to back side of four large squares.
9. Place Box inside four squares.
10. Give Box height of 5.
11. Use Lift arrow to lift table top by 15 to top of legs.
12. Highlight all.
13. Group all.
14. Done!

Step-by-Step

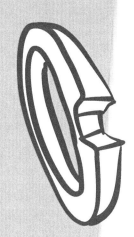

1. Under Basic Shapes, put a Tube on the Workplane.
2. Make it 50x50x5.
3. Increase Sides to 64 to make it smoother.
4. Put a Roof on the Workplane.
5. Rotate Roof 90 degrees towards the back to an upright position, with base of the Roof facing Front.
6. Make the Roof's bottom 8x8.
7. Move the Roof to top of Tube, lining up Black Center Points of both Tube and Roof.
8. Make Roof a Hole.
9. Highlight both.
10. Group....Done!

3D Recipes

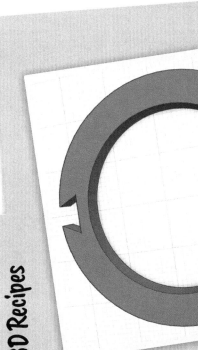

Ring

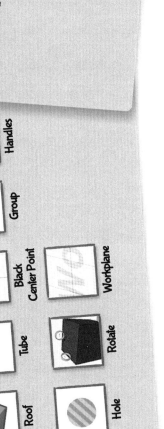

Roof   Tube   Black Center Point   Group   Handles

Hole   Rotate   Workplane

3D Recipes

Building

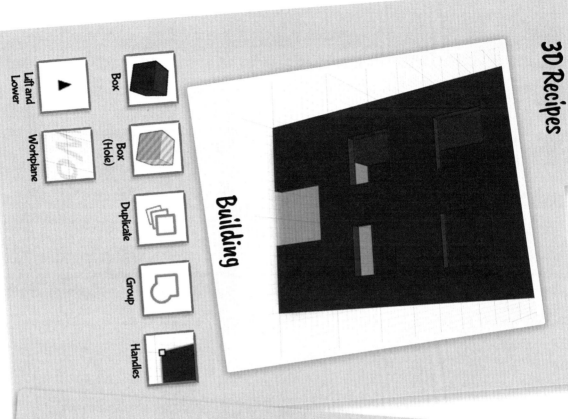

Box

Box (Hole)

Duplicate

Group

Handles

Lift and Lower

Step-by-Step

1. Pick four large squares on Workplace; note the center line.
2. Place Box Hole inside four squares.
3. Use Handle, hold down Shift, make 5x5x5 box at one corner of four large squares.
4. Slide Box Hole to two small squares to the left of the center line.
5. Duplicate.
6. Move duplicate Box Hole to two small squares to the right of the center line.
7. Highlight both.
8. Use Lift Arrow to lift by 10.
9. Duplicate.
10. Use Lift Arrow to lift duplicate by 20.
11. Place another Box Hole inside original four squares.
12. Use Handle, hold down Shift, make a 6x6x6 box for door.
13. Line up door on center line.
14. Place another Box Hole inside four squares.
15. Use Handle to change bottom to 18x18.
16. Place this large box at the center of four squares; use the drop line in the middle.
17. Make height of this Box Hole 28.
18. Place a solid Box inside four squares.
19. Give Box height of 30.
20. Highlight all; Group.
21. Done!

Step-by-Step

1. Pick four large squares on Workplace; note the center line.

2. Place a Cone inside four squares; increase Sides to smooth it.

3. Use Handle, hold down Shift, make it 18x18.

4. Use arrows to re-center this Cone in middle of four squares.

5. Click Hole to make it a hole.

6. Place a new Cone on top of the Cone Hole; increase Sides to smooth it.

7. Highlight both and Group.

8. Rotate 180 degrees.

9. Lift 10.

10. Place Paraboloid in center of four large squares.

11. Highlight both.

12. Group....Done!

3D Recipes

Cup

Cone	Paraboloid	Group	Handles	Hole

Lift and Lower	Rotate	Workplane

3D Recipes

Heart-shaped Box

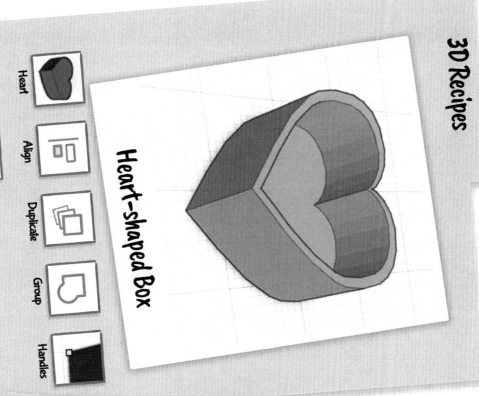

Heart

Align

Duplicate

Group

Handles

Hole

Lift and Lower

Step-by-Step

1. Under Basic Shapes, put a Heart on the Workplane.
2. Make it 20x20x3 where 3 is the height.
3. Duplicate it; move the copy to one side.
4. Return to first Heart and increase height to 10.
5. Duplicate.
6. Use Lift tool to raise the Duplicate by 2 from Workplane.
7. Use Handle of elevated Duplicate heart and make it 18x18 along bottom.
8. Highlight top and bottom Hearts and click Align tool.
9. Center Align front and side; click anywhere on Workplane to escape Align.
10. Make top Heart a Hole.
11. Highlight top and bottom Hearts and Group.
12. Go to Heart on the side to make cover.
13. Duplicate and raise Duplicate heart by 1 from Workplane.
14. Give elevated Duplicate 17.8x17.8 size along bottom.
15. Highlight top and bottom Heart and click Align tool.
16. Center Align front and side; click anywhere on Workplane.
17. Highlight both and Group.
18. Select color of choice and Done!

Step-by-Step

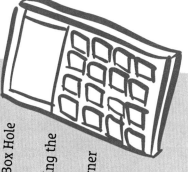

1. Place Ruler on Workplane, where two heavy lines meet.

2. Make sure you have enough space on the Workplane on the upper right.

3. Place a solid Box where its lower left corner meets Ruler's Origin.

4. Holding down Shift, click upper right Handle, pull in to make Box 5x5x5.

5. Duplicate Box.

6. Use Right Arrow key to slide Box to right by 10.

7. Click Duplicate two more times to create two more Boxes on right.

8. Highlight all four Boxes and click Duplicate.

9. Use Up Arrow key to slide four Boxes up by 10.

10. Click Duplicate two more times for a total of 16 Boxes.

11. Orbit and place Box Hole along line above 16 Boxes.

12. Make Box Hole 35x20 on bottom.

13. Orbit again, use the Lift tool and raise Box Hole height to 2.

14. Move Ruler Origin 5 left and 5 down using the small squares in Workplane.

15. Place a solid Box where its lower left corner meets Ruler's new Origin.

16. Make Box 70x45x4. Dismiss Ruler.

17. Highlight all; Group.

18. Done!

3D Recipes

Toy Phone

Handles

Group

Duplicate

Workplane

Box (Hole)

Ruler

Box

Lift and Lower

Step-by-Step

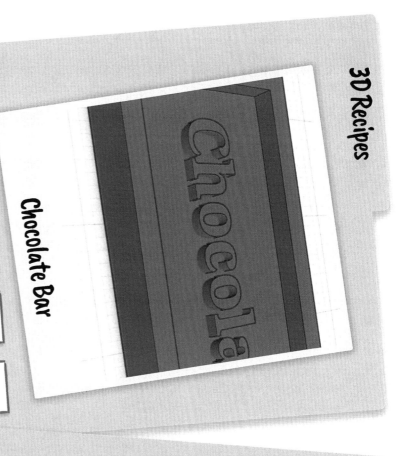

Chocolate Bar

Handles

Box

Box (Hole)

Lift and Lower

Text

Ruler

Align

Group

1. Place a Ruler anywhere on Workplane.
2. Place a Box anywhere and make it 40x20x4.
3. Place a Box Hole anywhere and make it 36x16x20.
4. Use Lift tool and raise the Box Hole by 2.
5. Highlight both.
6. Center Align on left side and bottom center. Click Workplane to exit Align.
7. Highlight both and Group.
8. Under Basic Shapes, place Text on Workplane. Type "Chocolate!!" and make it 30x5x3.
9. Highlight word and bar.
10. Center Align on bottom, side and vertically.
11. Dismiss Ruler.
12. Highlight all.
13. Group...Done!

3D Recipes

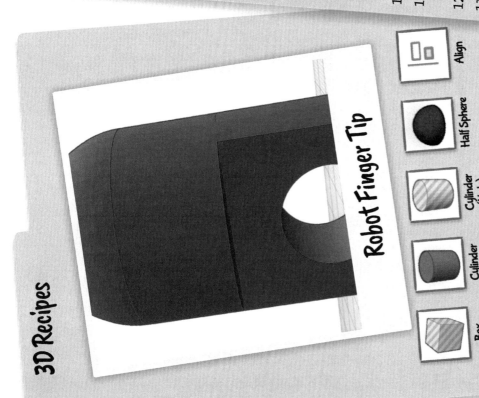

Robot Finger Tip

Box (Hole) | Cylinder | Cylinder (Hole) | Half Sphere | Align

Black Center Point | Duplicate | Group | Rotate | Workplane

Step-by-Step

1. Place a solid Cylinder at center of four large squares in Workplane, making sure Cylinder's Black Center Point lines up with heavy line on Workplane.

2. Increase Sides to 64 to smooth out the Cylinder.

3. Place Box Hole so bottom left corner falls on Cylinder's Black Center Point.

4. Use Right Arrow key to move Box Hole 5 units to right of Cylinder's Black Center Point.

5. Duplicate Box Hole and use arrow keys to move new Box Hole 5 units to left of Cylinder's Black Center Point.

6. Highlight all, Group.

7. Place Cylinder Hole on Workplane; Sides to 64, make it 10x10 on bottom.

8. Rotate 90 degrees to flat position.

9. Highlight all; Center Align on X, Y and Z axis; click Workplane to exit Align.

10. Highlight all and Group.

11. Place new solid Cylinder on Workplane; Sides to 64; height of 10; Lift 20.

12. Place Half Sphere on Workplane; Lift 30.

13. Highlight all; center Align on bottom and side; click outside to exit Align.

14. Highlight all.

15. Group....Done!

3D Recipes

Rocket

Handles

Cylinder | **Paraboloid** | **Wedge** | **Align** | **Group**

Mirror | **Workplane**

Step-by-Step

1. Under Basic Shapes, put a Wedge on Workplane.

2. Give it a depth of 11 and width of 2; height of fin faces Front.

3. Line up Black Center Point of fin's width to heavy line on Workplane.

4. Place fin to cover 10 small squares with remainder spilling over into large square.

5. Duplicate fin; use down arrow key to slide across two large squares to the Front.

6. Mirror tool to flip front fin so both height of fins face each other, with 18 small squares between them.

7. Highlight both; Duplicate; Rotate two fins 90 degrees; click outside.

8. Highlight all four fins; Group.

9. Put Cylinder on Workplane; Slide to 64 to smooth; Height of 70.

10. Put Paraboloid on Workplane; Lift tool to raise by 70.

11. Highlight all; use Align tool to center align on bottom two sides.

12. Highlight all.

13. Group....Done!

Step-by-Step

1. Under Basic Shapes, put a Wedge on the Workplane.
2. Rotate it 90 degrees so that the Wedge's back faces right.
3. Give it length of 100.
4. Put Round Roof on Workplane; give it height of 5.
5. Position Round Roof towards the back of the car body.
6. Use Lift tool to raise Round Roof higher than car body.
7. Highlight both; center Align along car length.
8. Rotate Round Roof 11 degrees counterclockwise.
9. Place Workplane tool on top of car body.
10. Click Round Roof; press D to drop.
11. Grab another Workplane tool and place it back to original level.
12. Highlight both; Group.
13. Orbit to front of car; Line up front left corner of car to corner of large square in Workplane.
14. Under Basic Shapes, place Tube, 2 large squares from front of car.
15. Increase Sides to 64; Wall Thickness of 8; Ensure Black Center Point lines up with heavy line.
16. Rotate tire 90 degrees upright.
17. Duplicate tire; move to car right side; ensure Black Center Point lines up with car body.
18. Holding down Shift key, Group both tires.
19. Highlight and Duplicate both tires; slide back to behind the Round Roof.
20. Highlight all; Use Lift tool to raise car above Workplane; press D to drop...Done!

3D Recipes

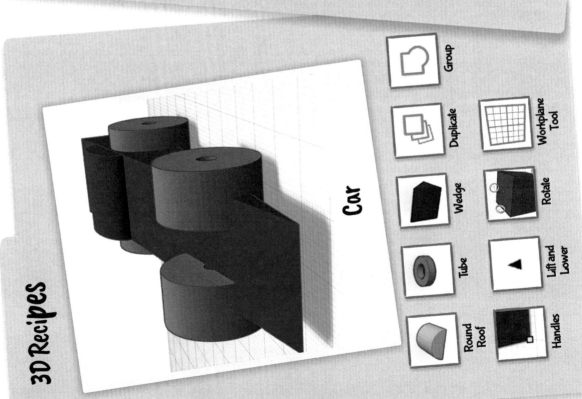

Car

Round Roof

Tube

Wedge

Duplicate

Group

Handles

Lift and Lower

Rotate

Workplane Tool

3D Recipes

Cylinder Star Align Group Snap Grid

Grid Edit 1.0

Wand

Step-by-Step

1. Under Basic Shapes, put a Star on the Workplane.
2. Rotate the Star 18 degrees counterclockwise so the bottom tips of the star line up with a horizontal line.
3. Give Star a height of 7.
4. Under Basic Shapes, put a Cylinder on the Workplane.
5. For Cylinder, increase Sides to 64; make bottom 6x6; give height of 70.
6. Orbit to side view; rotate Cylinder 90 degrees; press D to drop.
7. Slide one end of Cylinder into Star.
8. Highlight both; center Align along the length.
9. At Snap Grid on bottom right, select 0.5mm.
10. Use Lift tool to raise Cylinder by 0.5mm.
11. Highlight both.
12. Group...Done!

Appendix C:
Additional Resources

Tinkercad Classroom Introduction
https://blog.tinkercad.com/2019/08/05/introducing-tinkercad-classroom/

Tinkercad Classroom FAQ
https://tinkercad.zendesk.com/hc/en-us/articles/360026236693-Tinkercad-Classrooms

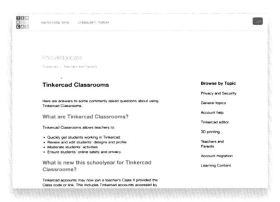

Cura Slicer Discussion Forum
https://community.ultimaker.com/forum/108-ultimaker-cura/

Appendix D:
Glossary of Key
3D Printing Terms

Extruder

Also called the print head, the extruder is where all the 3D printing action takes place. It's where the plastic is melted (at a very hot 200C (392F)) as it is placed in a very specific location on the print bed of your 3D printer. Several small stepper motors move the extruder left/right, forwards/backwards, and up/down as your printer is creating your 3D print. Because children are involved, it's very important to tell them not to touch the extruder when running.

Filament

For most education use, the filament of choice is polylactic acid, commonly known as PLA. It's considered to be biodegradable although there is some controversy surrounding that claim. Nevertheless, PLA is more eco-friendly than it's oil-based competitor, acrylonitrile butadiene styrene or ABS, which has lost its popularity in recent years. PLA comes in many different colors, is relatively inexpensive (ranging from US$15-25/1kg (2.2lbs)), has been standardized at a 1.75mm diameter, and is often sold in large spools, which makes it easy to use for most 3D printers.

After you open its air-sealed packaging, one shortfall for PLA is it becomes a little brittle after a long time in storage, say, more than a year. The brittleness doesn't make the filament unusable because as long as the filament is advancing towards the extruder, it will melt and become part of the 3D print. However, loading filament into the 3D printer that breaks easily is a bit annoying. So try to cycle through your filament on a regular basis.

G-Code

This is the file which your 3D printer needs in order to produce your print. Remember, after you create your 3D design, you need to export it as an STL file. Take this STL file and further prepare it in your slicer which will produce the G-code file that gets sent to your 3D printer.

Infill

Since 3D prints have an internal space (think of the space inside a simple box), it usually needs to be filled with something. This is called the infill. Infill can actually be just empty space, which might make the model a bit fragile, or it can also be filled completely with filament, which will extend the print time by several magnitudes and likely waste plastic. Infill percentages in the 5-20% range are popular because they strike a sufficient balance between empty, fragile prints and solid, potentially wasteful ones. Most slicing software can automatically create triangular or honeycomb patterns as infill to help provide support to the overall structure.

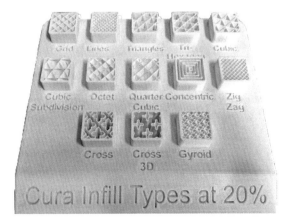

Infill Types - Design and photo courtesy Christopher Carbonneau

Print Bed

The print bed is the surface where all the 3D prints are made. Because the extruder is depositing the filament on its surface, it's vitally important the print bed stays level and consistent at every deposit point. Warped or slanted print beds will always result in failed 3D prints. Slanted print beds can be leveled out using thumb wheels under the print bed. Some print beds are made of glass or aluminum which can be heated to help the filament stick consistently during printing. When all else fails, try glue sticks (my personal preference), hair spray or blue printing tape.

Slicer

A slicer is a software which takes your 3D design and converts it from an STL file to a G-Code file for your 3D printer. (Your 3D printer can't understand an STL file.) Some 3D printers have their own slicer software. Many printers use open sourced, freely available slicers such as Cura. If you want more control of your 3D printer, consider buying slicers like Simplify3D for US$150. At the most basic level, when you load your 3D models into a slicer, you can define 1) the overall size of each 3D print; 2) the placement of each print on the print bed and 3) how hollow or filled in your models should be (The higher this in-fill setting, the longer your print time). However, other settings, like how wide the base of each print should be (to improve adhesion to the print bed), side wall and bottom layer thicknesses are also available.

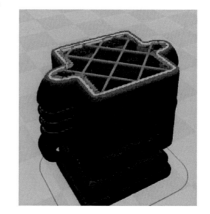

STL File

STL stands "stereo-lithography," a file format for 3D models. When you are ready to 3D print your design, export the model as an STL file to your desktop or some suitable file storage area. Open this STL file in your Slicer for further processing.

Support Material

Support material is tear away plastic material your slicer software included during the print because your model had overhanging sections. Imagine a student designed an upright humanoid robot with an outstretched arm. If there was no support material printed under the arm, the extruder would be spewing out filament in mid air when it reaches the point of printing the arm. The support material, which is thinner than the rest of the model, provides, as the name clearly states, support so that the arm can be made.

Index

Symbols
3D Printer Tools List 35
3D printing service 23, 24, 39

A
adjustable foot pegs 36
Autodesk 1, 12

B
baby wipes 34
blue tape 35, 37
bowls of spaghetti 39

C
chef 2, 41
classroom setup 5, 8–11
cleaning needle 39
clogging 38
CR-10S 34
Cura 26, 219, 222

D
default settings 29

E
extruder 33, 34, 35, 36, 38, 39, 220, 222, 223
extruder assembly 39

F
filament spools 33
floaters 27

G
G-code 221
glue stick 34, 35

H
hair spray 35, 37, 222

I
infill 221
ingredients 2, 2, 5

J
jam 36, 39

L
level the bed 36

M
maintenance 34
MakerBot 24, 38

N
needle nose pliers 35
nozzle 39

O
Octoprint 38
oven 2, 5, 30

P
paper sheet thickness test 36
pocket knife 33, 35
Printing Service 39
Printrbot Jr 39

R
recipes 9, 203
repairs 34

S
setup and use 5, 30
slicer 26, 29, 221, 222, 223
slicing 35, 221
slicing software 221
spatula 33, 35
STL 23
STL file 221, 222, 223
support material 33, 34, 35, 37, 223

T
tennis ball 28, 30
Tinkercad 1, 5, 9, 12, 13, 15, 16, 17, 18, 23, 24, 42, 45, 47, 123, 219

W
webcam 38

Key Tools Cheatsheet

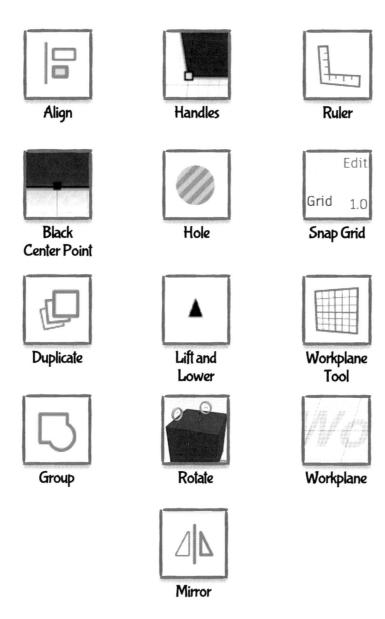

Align	Handles	Ruler
Black Center Point	Hole	Snap Grid
Duplicate	Lift and Lower	Workplane Tool
Group	Rotate	Workplane
	Mirror	

Basic Shapes Cheatsheet

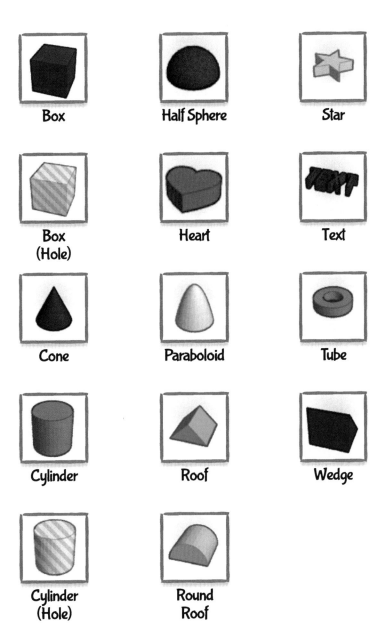

Box	Half Sphere	Star
Box (Hole)	Heart	Text
Cone	Paraboloid	Tube
Cylinder	Roof	Wedge
Cylinder (Hole)	Round Roof	